FINANCING THE EU BUDGET

FINANCING THE EU BUDGET
MOVING FORWARD OR BACKWARDS?

GABRIELE CIPRIANI

Published by Rowman & Littlefield International, Ltd.
Unit A, Whitacre Mews, 26-34 Stannary Street, London SE11 4AB
www.rowmaninternational.com

Rowman & Littlefield International, Ltd. is an affiliate of Rowman & Littlefield
4501 Forbes Boulevard, Suite 200, Lanham, Maryland 20706, USA
With additional offices in Boulder, New York, Toronto (Canada), and Plymouth (UK)
www.rowman.com

Centre for European Policy Studies
Place du Congrès 1, B-1000 Brussels
Tel: (32.2) 229.39.11 Fax: (32.2) 219.41.51
E-mail: info@ceps.eu
Website: http://www.ceps.eu

The right of Gabriele Cipriani to be identified as the author of this work has
been asserted by him in accordance with the Copyright, Designs and Patents
Act 1988. The opinions expressed by the author in this publication in no way
commit the European Court of Auditors to which he belongs.

Cover drawing: © Luigi Ripari (2010)

British Library Cataloguing in Publication Data
A catalogue record for this book is available from the British Library

ISBN 978-1-78348-330-3

Library of Congress Cataloging-in-Publication Data Available

In memory of Massimo Vari,
with respect, gratitude and affection

NOTE TO THE READER ON THE BOOK'S STRUCTURE

This study contains three chapters. Chapter 1 presents an historical overview of the EU revenue system. It examines the context for setting revenue arrangements and the concept of EU 'own resources'. This chapter further illustrates the implications of 'budgetary balances' calculations (i.e. the difference between member states' contributions to the EU budget and payments received from it), conceptual weaknesses and an alternative way to assess economic benefits induced by EU expenditure. The burden-sharing for financing the EU budget is examined in detail in the last section, accompanied by figures and tables with reference to member states and on a per capita basis.

Chapter 2 provides an assessment of the current system against simplicity, transparency, equity and democratic accountability. It examines the drawbacks of the proposals for reform put forward by the European Commission in 2011. It further discusses the potential for increasing public revenue represented by the significant amount of uncollected value-added tax (VAT). Finally, it sketches two possible options for reforming the EU revenue system, one 'member state-centred' and the other through a VAT-based resource levied directly on citizens.

The final chapter examines issues connected to EU revenue, such as the need to ensure its legitimacy through a demonstration of the added value of EU expenditure and a better rationale for setting the overall resources for the EU budget, on the basis of an assessment of the costs involved for achieving the intended results by each of the programmes.

CONTENTS

List of Figures

List of Tables

PREFACE

The on-going review of the EU revenue system by a High-Level Group on Own Resources, formed in February 2014 under the chairmanship of the former Italian Prime Minister and European Commissioner Mario Monti, is the last in a series of efforts at reform. This system, which is mostly based on member states' financial transfers, seems unalterable. Yet, it guarantees the resources needed to fund the around €140 billion spent each year by the EU budget. Why then change it?

The need for reform is implicit in the four criteria set for the review: simplicity, transparency, equity and democratic accountability. The current system does not score well against any of these criteria. In particular, while the EU budget is financed from the cashbox of overall national taxation, this is not made visible to taxpayers. Citizens are therefore left in the dark. Out of sight, out of mind.

The EU revenue system is an element of the legitimacy of the Union's action. In particular, the principles of transparency and taxation by consent would require making it possible for citizens to understand how the EU budget is financed and to ascertain what individual contributions they are making to fund it.

Funding the EU budget with a visible resource, which would represent a major political decision with no practical possible reversal, is the 'elephant in the room' faced by the review. On the one hand, it would offer a way to bring Europe closer to its citizens, acknowledging the status of the EU as a union of member states and their nationals. On the other hand, it would imply making citizens directly liable for funding the EU budget, while EU revenue arrangements have traditionally been regarded as the game preserves of national chancelleries.

Furthermore, raising awareness among EU citizens on their contribution to the EU budget will most likely stir up a volley of questions: What is the purpose of the EU budget? Who profits from it? On whom does the burden fall? Who is managing EU expenditure and who is ultimately accountable for the results? Thus, the visibility of EU revenue could prompt an unprecedented debate about the EU budget, and ultimately about the European integration process itself.

Should this possible line of questioning give EU policy-makers cause to be afraid to introduce visibility into the EU revenue process? The answer depends on how confident the EU institutions and member states feel that they can convincingly explain to EU citizens what the EU budget is for, what it has achieved so far and what it can further achieve in their interest and, finally, that all this is worth the cost.

Gabriele Cipriani
October 2014

Not everything that counts can be counted,
and not everything that can be counted counts.

Albert Einstein

1. THE EU BUDGET REVENUE SYSTEM

The EU revenue system should be considered in the context of the highly innovative and evolutionary nature of the European Union, which is neither an international organisation nor a federal state. Originating from the decision by its member states to pool selected aspects of their respective sovereignties, the EU's powers are founded on the principle of representation of interests.

The EU framework is based on a dual legitimacy, which "brings together states and peoples via a unique form of political integration",[1] in a process of governance 'without government' organised around a single institutional framework. The European Union constitutes a new legal order of international law, the subjects of which comprise not only member states but also their nationals.

The EU revenue system has been a subject of intense debate for years, in particular concerning the nature of the resources financing the EU budget. Many academicians have provided detailed reviews of the functioning and peculiarities of the system and have formulated a number of proposals to address its drawbacks. Still, the EU revenue system seems unalterable. In particular, no satisfactory solution has been found to make visible to citizens their contribution to the EU budget (some €140 billion in 2013, or an average of almost €280 per capita).

EU revenue: A short history

The evolution of the EU budget financing can be charted along the following timeline.

---

[1] See European Commission, "A project for the European Union", COM (2002) 247, Brussels, 22 May 2002, p. 20.

1952-1969. The European Coal and Steel Community (ECSC, 1951, Treaty of Paris) was entitled to procure the funds necessary to carry out its tasks by setting levies on the production of coal and steel, which might be defined as the first Community tax (Article 49 ECSC). By contrast, the Treaty of Rome (EEC, 1957) provided that the budget of the European Economic Community would be initially financed from member states' contributions (Article 200 EEC), as shown in Table 1, with the option of replacing them by Community's own resources at a later stage (Article 201 EEC).

Member states' contributions were based on a percentage scale provided for in the Treaty, differentiated according to the type of expenditure (administrative or operational). These scales were the result of a political agreement, although close to countries' share in gross domestic product (GDP) at that time. The Council was entitled to modify the scales, by unanimous agreement. This happened notably in order to fund agricultural spending.

Table 1. Share of the EEC budget financing by founding member states (%)

Member states	Administrative expenditure (%)	Social Fund (%)
Belgium	7.9	8.8
Germany	28	32
France	28	32
Italy	28	20
Luxembourg	0.2	0.2
Netherlands	7.9	7
	100	100

Source: Article 200 of the EEC Treaty.

1970-1984. In 1970, after long and difficult negotiations, member states agreed that "the Communities shall be allocated resources of their own" and that "from 1 January 1975 the budget of the Communities shall, irrespective of other revenue, be financed entirely from the Communities' own resources".[2] As a result, from 1971, customs duties, agricultural duties, and

---

[2] See Articles 1 and 4 of Council Decision 70/243/ECSC, EEC, Euratom of 21 April 1970 on the replacement of financial contributions from member states by the

sugar and isoglucose levies (called 'Traditional own resources' or TOR) collected at EU entry were gradually transferred to the EU budget. In order to cover the administrative expenses for their collection, 10% of TOR was retained by the member states. Member states' contributions from the value added tax (VAT)-based resource (1% of the taxable base) were made in full for the first time in 1980, covering around 50% of EU expenditure.

1985-1987. The call-up rate for the VAT-based resource was increased from 1% to 1.4% and the principle was formalised that any member state bearing an excessive budgetary burden in relation to its relative prosperity may benefit at the appropriate time from a correction. A correction was granted to the United Kingdom (the UK rebate), in the form of a reduction of its VAT-based resource payments, to be financed by the other member states (with Germany paying two-thirds of its share).

1988-1994. The principle of a multiannual financial framework (MFF) was introduced as a budgetary planning tool. Appropriations for payments were set by a global ceiling expressed as a percentage of member states' total gross national product (GNP), increasing from 1.15% for 1988 to 1.20% for 1992. A new resource was levied at a uniform rate in proportion to the GNP of each member state, as a measure of a country's prosperity.[3] The GNP-based resource was also meant to function as a 'top-up' source of revenue to balance the budget, thus guaranteeing sufficient funding for the EU budget. In addition, while the maximum call-up rate for the VAT-based resource was maintained at 1.4%, member states' VAT base was capped at a percentage (55%) of each national GNP. The reason invoked was to counter an alleged regressive effect of the VAT-based resource with relatively less well-off member states.[4]

Communities' own resources (OJ No L 94 of 28 April 1970, p. 19). Member states' contributions for the transitional period until 31 December 1974 were fixed as follows: Belgium (6.8%), Germany (32.9%), France (32.6%), Italy (20.2%), Luxembourg (0.2%) and the Netherlands (7.3%).

[3] GNP results from adding to GDP the compensation of employees and the property income received from the rest of the world and by deducting the corresponding flows paid to the rest of the world.

[4] The percentage of capping of the VAT base does not result from any specific criteria. In particular, the size of the VAT base and therefore the effect of the capping is not proportional to member states' GNP/GNI. Gros & Micossi (2005:12) challenged the traditional view about a regressive effect of the VAT resource, by

1995-1999. The global own resources ceiling for payments was increased (from 1.21% for 1995 to 1.27% for 1999). There was also a progressive broadening of the capping of the VAT base (50% in 1999 for all member states) and a lowering of the call-up rate for the VAT-based resource (from 1.32% in 1995 to 1.0% in 1999).

2000-2006. GNP was replaced by the concept of gross national income (GNI).[5] The global own resources ceiling for payments was slightly decreased (from 1.07% of GNI for 2000 to 1.06% for 2006). The maximum call-up rate for the VAT-based resource was reduced from 1% to 0.75% in 2002 and 2003 and to 0.50% from 2004 onwards. Starting with the calculation of the UK rebate in 2001, Austria, Germany, the Netherlands and Sweden obtained to fund this rebate to a quarter of their normal share. As from 2001, the percentage of TOR that member states retain to cover collection costs was increased from 10% to 25%.

2007-2013. The global own resources ceiling for payments was set at 1.23% of GNI. The uniform rate of call of the VAT-based resource was reduced to 0.30%, although with some exceptions (for Austria it was fixed at 0.225%, for Germany at 0.15% and for the Netherlands and Sweden at 0.10%). A gross annual reduction in their GNI contribution was granted to the Netherlands (€605 million) and Sweden (€150 million).

2014-2020. While the global own resources ceiling for payments remains at 1.23% of GNI, the actual amount of payment appropriations has been lowered by almost 4% compared to the previous period. Reduced VAT-based resource rates (0.15% rather than 0.30% for the other member states) are applied to Germany, the Netherlands and Sweden. Moreover, Denmark,

---

observing that among countries with high VAT revenues one finds both rich (Sweden) and poor (Hungary); the same applies to countries with low VAT revenues in proportion to GDP (e.g. Spain, a Cohesion country, and Italy, with GDP per capita above the EU average). A factual analysis undertaken by the Commission in 2011 came to similar conclusions. It shows in particular that the slight negative relationship between potential VAT revenues, expressed as a % of GNI, and the GNI per capita of the member states, seems not to be statistically significant and in some cases could be partly due to other factors (see European Commission, Financing the EU budget: Report on the operation of the own resources system, SEC (2011) 876 of 27 October 2011, Brussels, p. 15 and p. 27).

[5] GNI equals GDP minus primary income payable by resident institutional units to non-resident institutional units plus primary income receivable by resident institutional units from the rest of the world.

the Netherlands and Sweden will benefit from reductions of their national GNI payments of €130 million, €695 million and €185 million, respectively. The Austrian annual GNI contribution will be reduced by €30 million in 2014, €20 million in 2015 and €10 million in 2016. Finally, TOR collection costs retained by member states are reduced from 25% to 20%.[6]

Figure 1 traces the evolution of the resources financing the EU budget since 1970.[7]

Figure 1. The composition of EU revenue – Selected years (outturn, %)

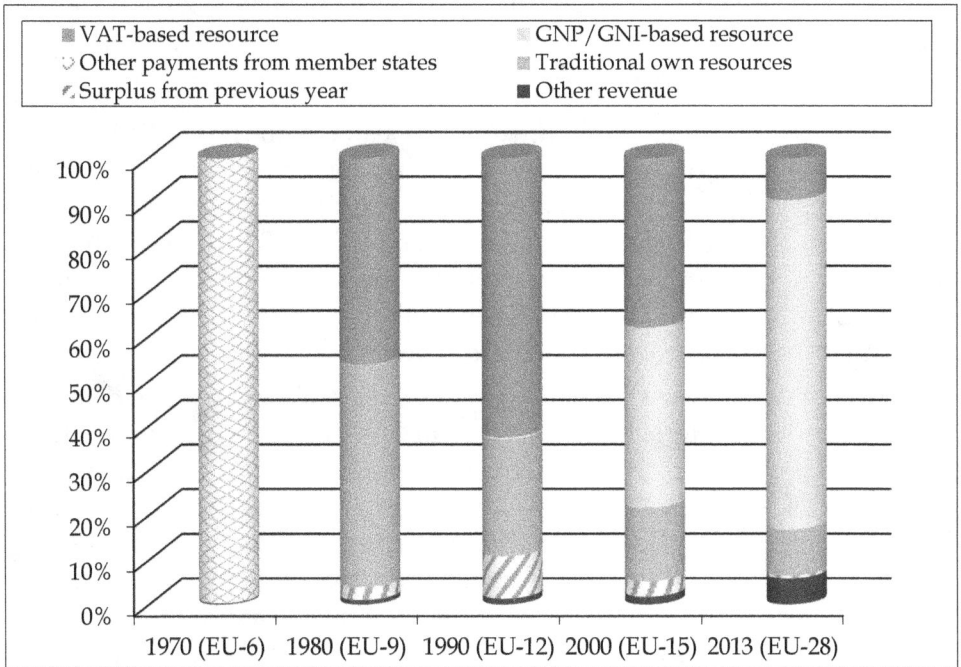

Source: Author's own elaboration from European Commission – EU budget financial reports for 2007 and 2013, Luxembourg, 2008 and 2014.

[6] See Council Decision of 26 May 2014 (2014/335/EU, Euratom) on the system of own resources of the European Union (OJ L 168 of 7 June 2014, p. 105). Its entering into force is subject to member states' ratification, which is currently in progress.

[7] Other sources of revenue contribute to the EU budget financing, such as a tax on EU staff salaries and pensions, contributions from non-EU countries to certain EU programmes (e.g. EFTA countries in the research area), repayment of unused EU financial assistance, interest on late payments, fines imposed for breaches of EU law. In 2013, such revenue was close to €9 billion. It should also be noted that as the outturn of the previous exercise is normally a surplus (around €1.5 billion in 2011, and €1 billion in 2012 and 2013), member states' contributions in the subsequent year are reduced correspondingly.

The figure shows that the pattern of revenue has undergone a profound modification over the years. This is principally due to the emergence of the GNP/GNI-based resource (74% of the own resources for the period 2007-2013) at the expense of the VAT-based resource, but also to the reduction of customs duties following the trade liberalisation and the increase of collection costs paid to member states as from 2001. Initially intended to complement the existing own resources, the GNP/GNI-based resource has become the dominant source of revenue as a conventional indicator of the contributive capacity of individual member states.

What do 'own resources' actually mean?

Following Article 3(6) of the Treaty on European Union (TEU), "[t]he Union shall pursue its objectives by appropriate means commensurate with the competences which are conferred upon it in the Treaties". Article 311 of the Treaty on the functioning of the European Union (TFEU) further clarifies that "[t]he Union shall provide itself with the means necessary to attain its objectives and carry through its policies. Without prejudice to other revenue, the budget shall be financed wholly from own resources".[8]

It should be noted that the EEC founding Treaty provided for the Community budget to be financed in a first phase through member states' contributions (Article 200 EEC), with possibly moving on to the Community's 'own resources' at a later stage (Article 201 EEC). Thus, the Treaty of Rome set a clear distinction between these two types of funding sources. This transition, ensured in principle by the decision of 21 April 1970 "on the replacement of financial contributions from Member States by the Communities' own resources", provided the political justification for giving the European Parliament budgetary powers.[9]

As observed by Ehlermann (1982:572, 584-585), the exceptional procedure required for adopting such a decision (unanimity in Council plus ratification by national parliaments) was similar to that for introducing

---

[8] It should be added that Article 323 TFEU provides: "The European Parliament, the Council and the Commission shall ensure that the financial means are made available to allow the Union to fulfil its legal obligations in respect of third parties."

[9] While budgetary powers were previously vested in the Council alone, a gradual increase in the Parliament's powers was endowed by the Treaties of 22 April 1970 and of 22 July 1975. In particular, Parliament was given the last word on 'not compulsory' expenditure (see footnote 131), the power to adopt the budget and to grant discharge to the Commission for the budgetary implementation.

direct elections of the European Parliament (Article 138(3) EEC). This coincidence should be interpreted as the wish to make the EU financially independent from member states, just as direct elections of the European Parliament severed its 'umbilical cord' with national parliaments. Therefore, the purpose of these provisions would have been to disengage the Community progressively from the member states.

The concept of 'own resources' was therefore meant to imply a shift of sovereignty on the part of member states, allowing the Community to exert a direct power of taxation over EU citizens. In this respect, Strasser (1991:91) defined 'own resources' as a tax borne directly by EU taxpayers which is included under revenue in the EU general budget and does not appear in the budgets of the member states.

Yet, the idea that the EU is financed by resources that belong to it by right as a cornerstone of its financial autonomy, and that therefore revenue accrues automatically without the need for any subsequent decision by national authorities, needs to be put into context and its evolution considered over time. In particular, a key overarching element of the EU financing system is that EU expenditure is subject to strict predictability ('budgetary discipline'), ensured through three main features:

i.   The overall volume of EU revenue is limited (since 1988) by an 'own resources' ceiling (for the MFF 2014-2020, payments shall not exceed 1.23% of the EU GNI). This ceiling is updated every year on the basis of the latest forecasts in order to guarantee that the EU's total estimated level of payments does not exceed the maximum amount of own resources that the EU may raise during a given year.[10]

ii.   The EU budget is subject to the principle of equilibrium. This means in practice that to balance the budget each year, the revenue is determined in relation to the expenditure (and not the other way

---

[10] Moreover, the overall amount of funds resulting from the application of the own resources ceiling has to be referred to GNI as estimated under ESA 95. The 2014-2020 own resource decision (Council Decision of 26 May 2014, 'Whereas' 6 and Article 3, op. cit.) specifies that the entering into force of ESA 2010 (Regulation (EU) No 549/2013 of the European Parliament and of the Council of 21 May 2013, OJ L 174, 26 June 2013, p. 1), which replaces ESA 95 (and will result, due mainly to the capitalisation of expenditure on R&D and weapon systems, in an increase of EU GNI of more than 2%), should however not raise the overall amounts agreed by the MFF.

round). Unlike its member states, the EU is not allowed to borrow to finance its activities or to cover any budget deficit.[11]

iii.   To ensure at the same time that EU spending is predictable, the MFF plays the role of a budgetary planning tool, laying down the maximum annual amounts ('ceilings') for broad categories of expenditure over a period of at least 5 years.[12]

Therefore, as is often explained by the Commission, the EU budget cannot grow out of control. It never runs a deficit, never builds up debt and only spends what it receives. It is always balanced.

Moreover, the EU does not have the power to raise taxes on its own. The type, the nature and the overall amount of the own resources as well as accessory specific arrangements are dealt with by a decision (the own resources decision) adopted unanimously by the Council, after consultation with the European Parliament.[13] To enter into force, that decision requires further approval by each member state in accordance with its constitutional requirements, thus respecting national sovereignty. This implies in most cases a ratification by national parliaments; hence, the own resources decision constitutes a 'Treaty' within the Treaties. In practice, however,

---

[11] See Article 310(1) TFEU and Article 17 of the Financial Regulation (EU, EURATOM) No 966/2012 of the European Parliament and of the Council of 25 October 2012 (OJ No L 298 of 26 October 2012).

[12] The principle of an MFF is enshrined in the Treaties (Article 312 TFEU). The MFF Regulation is adopted by the Council (unanimously, although the possibility exists for the European Council to authorise its adoption by a qualified majority) in accordance with a special legislative procedure, on a proposal from the Commission and after obtaining the consent of the European Parliament. This means that Parliament can only adopt or reject the whole MFF, but has no genuine power of co-decision. For the 2014-2020 MFF, see Council Regulation (EU, EURATOM) No 1311/2013 of 2 December 2013, laying down the multiannual financial framework for the years 2014-2020 (OJ No L 347 of 20 December 2013, p. 884).

[13] This procedure reflects the respective budgetary powers of the European Parliament and of the Council, as laid down by Article 314 TFEU. Paragraph 10 of this Article states: "Each institution shall exercise the powers conferred upon it under this Article in compliance with the Treaties and the acts adopted there under, with particular regard to the Union's own resources and the balance between revenue and expenditure." However, Parliament's consent is required concerning the adoption of implementing measures for the system of the Union's own resources, which, inter alia, define the assessment basis of the resources (see Article 311 TFEU).

national parliaments are under considerable pressure to give a green light to an agreement negotiated and approved by their own governments. A denial would re-open a negotiation with no guarantee of a more favourable outcome for the member states concerned.

While the legal texts define all EU financing sources as 'own resources', only TOR revenue (13% of 'own resources' in the period 2007-2013) can be considered to be a 'true' EU financing source, since the EU is the legitimate institutional recipient of duties levied on a specific and identifiable taxable operation. Also, as there is often no coincidence between the place of collection and the final consumption of the goods, this revenue could not be attributed to a specific member state.

By contrast, the assessment basis of the VAT and GNI-based resources (87% of 'own resources' in the period 2007-2013) derive from a member states' calculation, mostly based on statistical data.[14] These resources are therefore not 'collected' but put at the disposal of the EU budget as financial transfers from the cashbox of overall national taxation. In particular, the VAT-based resource is not levied directly on national taxable persons (and therefore on consumers), but on member states' 'notional' harmonised VAT bases. In addition, due to the 'capping mechanism', the VAT-based resource has since 1988 become de facto a GNP/GNI-based resource for the countries

---

[14] For the VAT-based resource, the establishment of each member state's assessment base starts from the total net VAT revenue collected. The latter is divided by a 'weighted average rate', meant to represent the statistical weighting of each VAT rate in the various categories of taxable goods and services subject to VAT. This intermediate base is finally adjusted with negative or positive compensations in order to obtain the final harmonised VAT base on which the EU call rate is applied (for the origin and evolution of the VAT-based resource, see Cipriani, 2007, pp. 46-64). The GNI resource is obtained by the application of a rate determined within the budgetary procedure to the sum of all member states' GNI forecasts. Member states are bound to establish the aggregate in a manner consistent with the European System of National and Regional Accounts (ESA), currently ESA 2010. The calculations underlying the assessment basis for these resources are complex and give room to numerous and often long-standing 'reservations' by the Commission. These reservations relate to the methods used by the member states for determining the national accounts or specific aspects of the calculation of the VAT base. At the end of 2013, there were 288 reservations awaiting solution concerning the GNI-based resource and 108 reservations concerning the VAT-based resource.

concerned. In 2014, five member states (Croatia, Cyprus, Luxembourg, Malta and Slovenia) will have their VAT bases capped at 50% of their GNI.

Finally, member states' contributions to the EU budget are recorded in national budgets in a diverse way. Only very few countries attribute contributions to the EU budget directly as appropriations to the EU and thus as a reduction in income of the central government (notably France, Germany, Austria and Romania). The majority considers the contributions to the EU budget as government expenditures. The exception is for TOR, and at times the VAT-based resource, but even there practices vary.[15]

The discussion above shows that the 'relay' envisaged by the EEC Treaty between national contributions and 'own resources', with the latter meant to be a direct levy on citizens in view of making the EU financially independent, has not taken place. Member states have remained in the end the (pay)masters. Under the current circumstances, EU 'financial autonomy' means no more than member states' complying with the obligation they have set on themselves to finance each year the EU budget within the limits of the MFF-agreed ceiling.

To each its own

In a speech to the European Parliament, 11 January 1977, Roy Jenkins, then President of the European Commission, observed:

> To wish to benefit from the success of the Community is a very good thing. But what is quite different, and indeed highly undesirable, is constantly to try to strike a narrow arithmetical balance as to exactly how much day-to-day profit or loss each country is getting out of the Community. (...) The Community can and must be more than the sum of its parts. It can create and give more than it receives, but only if the Member States, people and governments alike, have the vision to ask what they can contribute, and not just what they can get.[16]

This statement provides good evidence of member states' longstanding practice to calculate the benefits accrued from EU expenditure

---

[15] See the study undertaken for the European Parliament's Committee on Budgets, "How do members states handle contributions to the EU budget in their national budgets", by Jørgen Mortensen, Jorge Núñez Ferrer and Federico Infelise, October 2014, p. 42.

[16] See R. Jenkins, Speech to the European Parliament, 11 January 1977.

as the difference between their contributions to and the receipts from the EU budget ('budgetary balances').

Figure 2 shows, for the period 2007-2013, the allocation of EU expenditure (total and by main spending areas) to the five main 'net-payer' member states (Germany, France, Italy, the United Kingdom and the Netherlands) as well as their 'operating budgetary balances'.[17] These member states fund together around two-thirds of national contributions to the EU budget.

Figure 2. Allocation of EU expenditure and 'operating budgetary balances' – selected member states (outturn 2007-2013, € million)

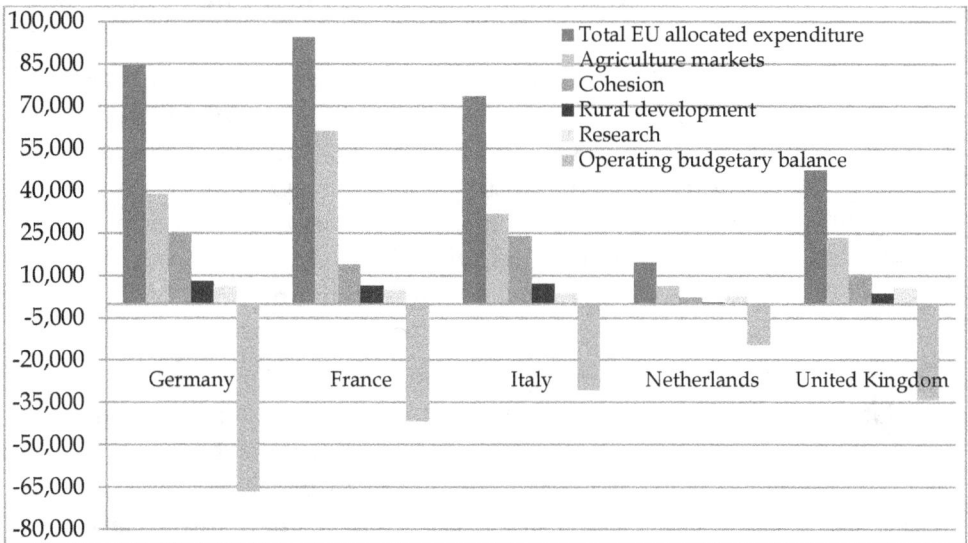

Source: Author's own elaboration based on European Commission, "EU Budget 2013 Financial Report", Luxembourg, 2014.

---

[17] Member states' 'operating budgetary balances' are calculated as the difference between their share in total 'national contributions' (VAT and GNI-based resources) paid to the EU and their share in the 'operating' expenditure (thus excluding Institutions' administrative expenditure) allocated to EU countries, multiplied by the total amount of the latter. As a result, the sum of all member states' balances adds up to zero. EU expenditure is allocated to the country in which the principal recipient resides, on the basis of the information available. Approximations and assumptions are sometimes necessary (for further details see http://ec.europa.eu/ budget/financialreport/annexes/annex3/index_en.html). The concept of budgetary balances draws a formal recognition since it is at the basis of the calculation of the UK rebate (see Article 4 of Council Decision of 26 May 2014, op. cit., COM (2014) 271 of 14 May 2014 and Council document 9823/14 of 15 May 2014).

Figure 2 shows that:

- Over the 2007-13 period, France has been the major beneficiary of EU expenditure. This is due to the fact that this country accounts for a high share of EU total 'agriculture markets' expenditure (21%) and that this spending area represents a significant proportion of total expenditure (some 37% for the MFF 2007-2013).

- As compared to other major member states like Germany, France and Italy, the United Kingdom has benefited from a lower amount of EU payments, overall and in general for the spending areas considered. Only for 'Research' spending does the United Kingdom record a relatively high position (in second place, behind Germany).

- The share of the United Kingdom in 'agriculture markets' expenditure is well below that of Italy, France and Germany. This situation, one of the grounds at the basis of the UK rebate, suggests that as long as expenditure related to agriculture market and direct payments to farmers will represent some 30% of the EU budget operational expenditure (2014-2020 MFF), the UK will most likely feel legitimated to keep claiming an imbalance in its disfavour.

It should be stressed that, as indicated by the Commission, the calculation of 'budgetary balances' is merely an accounting exercise of certain financial costs and benefits. It gives no indication of many of the other benefits gained from EU policies contributing to the far-reaching Union's objectives. The conventions that determine these calculations are 'arbitrary' and 'highly questionable'.[18] Yet, despite its conceptual weaknesses, 'budgetary balances' calculations have emerged as the key benchmark for the MFF negotiation. In this context, 'budgetary balances' provide to each member state a measure for negotiating the MFF in view of reaching an outcome that is politically defensible at home and to monitor its implementation during the programming period. In fact, EU expenditure represents the financial 'return' of national contributions paid to the EU. This explains that a large part of this expenditure (agricultural market-related expenditure and direct payments to farmers, rural development, fisheries

---

[18] See European Commission, SEC (2011) 876 of 27 October 2011, op. cit., p. 45.

and cohesion, representing some 70% of the 2014-2020 MFF) is directly or de facto pre-allocated on a country basis as part of the MFF deal.[19]

The problem is not that member states try to assess the benefits they get from the EU budget, but rather that they are using the 'wrong' measuring instrument. 'Budgetary balances' calculations are a way of assigning importance to what can be measured rather than measuring what is important. As shown in a previous study, assessing the economic impact of EU expenditure would need a different approach.[20] In this respect, it can be assumed that an EU payment triggers an increase in the demand of production of goods and/or services. This increased demand represents a meaningful *proxy* of the economic benefits generated by such payment. The increase in the demand of production will not be limited to the country where the beneficiary of the EU payment resides since, to be satisfied, the increase in the production will generate import flows from other countries (within/outside the EU). For example, EU funds disbursed to build a road investment in country X will trigger an increase of production also in the countries whose economic actors participate in the construction by providing workforce, materials and machinery.[21]

---

[19] It is worth noting, however, that for the Environment and Climate Action – LIFE – programme (€3.5 billion during 2014-2020), national allocations will apply only to the sub-programme 'Environment' and until 2017. From 2018 onwards, national allocations are phased out and the selection of projects will be based on relative merits.

[20] See Cipriani & Pisani (2004).

[21] As discussed in a previous study (Cipriani, 2007, section on "Estimating the benefits, a facile solution"), funding structural expenditure in less well-off countries can generate a significant economic return for richer countries. For example, after their accession to the EU, the value of imports of the EU-10 from the EU-15 rose significantly. As a result, the negative trade balance of the EU-10 for the period 2004–2006 was considerably higher compared with the period 2000–2003. It should also be noted that the value of EU funds for Cohesion and Rural Development allocated by the 2007-2013 MFF to the EU-10 member states represented around one-fifth of the value of imports of these countries from 'net-payer' countries (Belgium, France, Germany, Italy, the Netherlands, Austria, Sweden and the United Kingdom) in the previous seven years. Finally, the economic impact of EU expenditure beyond the recipient countries is recognised at the national level (for example by the United Kingdom) and also outside the EU, by EFTA countries, which enjoy a privileged access to the internal market.

The geographical allocation of the 'induced' production generated by EU payments can be estimated using an input-output model (based on Eurostat data) showing the magnitude of the inter-industry flows in terms of the levels of production in each sector. The underlying assumption is that all economic productive activities can be divided into sectors whose interrelations can be meaningfully expressed in a set of simple input functions.

An analysis of the economic impact of EU expenditure would therefore tell a different story than 'budgetary balances' calculations. While the latter imply that the accounting advantage of a member state comes at the expense of another member state, the economic reality would show a 'win-win' scenario as member states profit from EU expenditure, although to different degrees due to the diversity of the national industrial structures.

Table 2. Comparison of net balances calculated according to 'operating budgetary balances' and 'induced' production demand (2000-2002)

Member states	Net balance (€ million)		Ranking		
	Operating budgetary balances	Induced production demand	Operating budgetary balances	Induced production demand	Difference
(a)	(b)	(c)	(d)	(e)	(f = d - e)
Belgium	-299	1,364	7	8	-1
Denmark	-4	994	6	10	-4
Germany	-6,216	1,045	14	9	5
Greece	4,149	6,747	2	3	-1
Spain	7,504	17,552	1	1	0
France	-1,237	7,398	11	2	9
Ireland	1,531	4,043	4	7	-3
Italy	-894	4,497	10	5	5
Netherlands	-1,874	-331	13	14	-1
Austria	-345	381	8	12	-4
Portugal	2,253	5,574	3	4	-1
Finland	75	889	5	11	-6
Sweden	-863	-228	9	13	-4
UK	-1,270	4,221	12	6	6

Source: Cipriani & Pisani (2004).

Table 2 shows the final outcome of the exercise, through a comparison of two types of balances. The first balance (column b), in line with the traditional 'operating budgetary balances' approach, has been calculated by subtracting member states' payments to the EU budget (VAT and GNI-based resources) from EU payments received ('operating budgetary balance'). The second balance (column c) has been obtained by subtracting member states' payments to the EU budget (VAT and GNI-based resources) from the estimate of 'induced' production demand generated by EU payments.[22] Although the figures date back to the period 2000-2002, they provide an illustrative example of the differences that one may expect by using the two different approaches.

Not surprisingly, this comparison shows very different results according to the two types of balances, which can be summarised as follows:

- Countries appearing as 'net' contributors according to the 'operating budgetary balances' concept (for example, Belgium, Denmark, Germany, France, Italy, Austria and the United Kingdom) are in fact 'net' beneficiaries when taking into account the 'induced' demand.

- *Mutatis mutandis*, the same happens with countries that are traditionally 'net' beneficiaries like Spain. The value of the 'real' net balance for this country is more than two times higher than its 'budgetary' balance.

- The Netherlands and Sweden remain 'net' contributors in the two scenarios, although the deficit according to the 'induced' demand is rather limited compared to the one observed on the basis of 'operating budgetary balances'.

In order to highlight how each country changes its position in the hierarchy of 'net contributors', two rankings have been drawn up. The first is based on 'operating budgetary balances' (column d) and the second on the induced demand (column e). Both rankings are shown in descending order, placing in first place the country most advantaged and in 14th place the biggest 'net contributor'. Compared to the 'operating budgetary balances' ranking, four countries improve their relative position if the induced demand is taken into account (see column f). In this way, France recovers

---

[22] It should be stressed that the total amount of the estimated benefits, calculated following the methodology of the induced demand, is bigger than the EU expenditure (approximately +80%). This is due to the fact that the methodology considers not only the first productive cycle but also all subsequent iterations until the initial demand shock generated by EU payments is exhausted.

nine positions, the United Kingdom six, and Germany and Italy five each. Spain remains at the same level while all other member states would obtain a lower ranking.

Independently of the degree of precision of the numerical results (which are highly dependent on the accuracy and the reliability of the available statistical data), it seems established that when evaluating the benefits accruing from EU expenditure, 'budgetary balances' calculations provide a very limited, and in a way misleading, assessment.

An analysis of the economic impact of EU expenditure would also allow us to assess the likely 'geographical' effects of a possible different sectoral allocation of EU spending. Such an assessment could provide useful indications for addressing concerns of budgetary imbalances by some countries, in line with the 1984 Fontainebleau European Council Conclusions stressing that such imbalances should be ultimately addressed by means of expenditure policy.[23]

The price of unanimity

It is inherent to a revenue system based on 'national contributions' to be characterised by specific arrangements to reach the required member states' unanimous consent. Although not provided for by the Treaties, corrective measures were introduced in the 1980s "to solve, it was hoped, problems related to budgetary imbalances".[24] The best known is the UK rebate, agreed in June 1984 (European Council of Fontainebleau). The rebate consists of reducing by two-thirds the balance between the United Kingdom's contribution to the budget and EU payments to this country. The financial impact over time of the rebate is shown in Figure 3.

---

[23] See the Conclusions of the Fontainebleau European Council, 25-26 June 1984, point 1, and of the Berlin European Council, 24-25 March 1999, point 68.

[24] See European Commission, SEC (2011) 876 of 27 October 2011, op. cit., p. 10.

Figure 3. The amounts of the UK correction, 1984-2011 (€ billion and % of GNI)

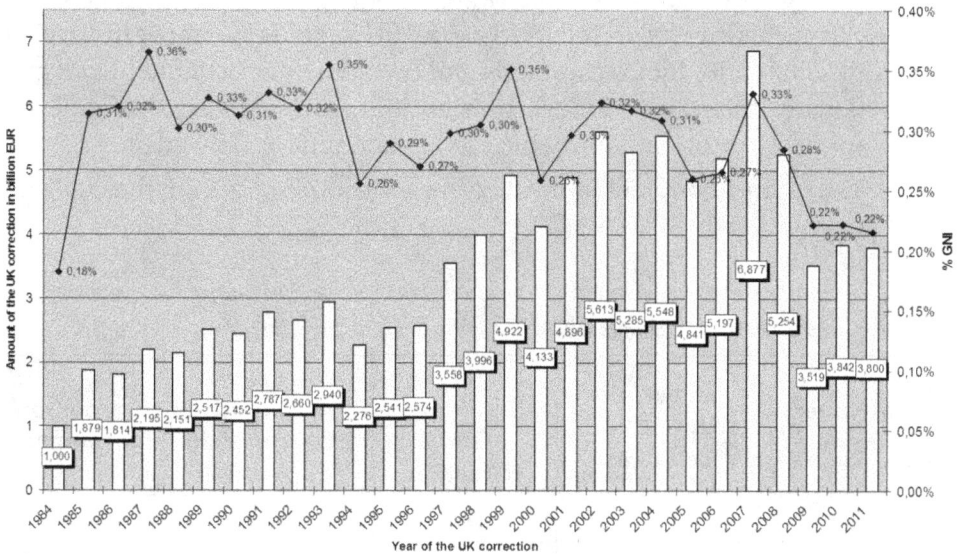

Note: The amounts of the UK correction for 2008-2011 are provisional.

Source: European Commission, "Financing the EU Budget: Report on the Operation of the Own Resources System", Commission Staff Working Paper, SEC (2011) 876 of 27 October 2011, p. 49.

The UK rebate has opened the floodgates of member states' claims to reduce their contributions on the basis of the same arguments, i.e. being too high compared to their relative wealth and the benefits they get out of the EU budget. These claims started with the financing of the UK rebate itself, as Germany was allowed to pay only two-thirds of its normal share, the balance being divided among the other member states. Later, also the Netherlands, Austria and Sweden have obtained a 'rebate' of their normal financing share.[25] Other forms of correction have been introduced over time. For example, the capping of member states' VAT bases at 50% of each national GNI, or the percentage of collection costs refunded to member states in

---

[25] As a result, in 2014, only 9% of the cost of the UK rebate (estimated at €5.3 billion) is borne by Germany, the Netherlands, Austria and Sweden. Most of the bill will be paid by France and Italy (27% and 20%, respectively). A further 31% is funded by member states whose GNI per capita (PPS) is below the EU average.

return for collecting TOR.[26] While these corrections have a permanent nature, other corrections have been agreed for the duration of a specific MFF. For example, as shown in section 1.1 on "EU revenue: A short history" for the MFF 2007-2013, the Netherlands and Sweden have benefited from gross reductions in their annual GNI contributions, and reduced VAT call rates were applied to Austria, Germany, the Netherlands and Sweden.

The financial impact of most corrections applied during the 2007-2013 MFF is provided in Table 3.

Table 3. Impact of correction mechanisms granted to Germany, the Netherlands, Austria and Sweden (draft budget 2012, € million)

Member state	Impact of reduced VAT call rates	Impact of lump sum GNI reduction	Impact of reduced share in UK correction financing	Combined impact
Germany	1,143. 7	- 174	681.1	1,650.9
Netherlands	437.7	638	160.4	1,236.1
Austria	38.9	- 20	76.6	95.6
Sweden	261.9	142	103.7	507.6

---

[26] The percentage of collection costs refunded to member states is an automatic entitlement, unrelated to the actual costs incurred. As observed by the Commission, such a high percentage does not correspond to actual collection costs and can be considered a hidden correction mechanism to allow certain member states to decrease their payments to the EU budget (see Commission Staff Working Paper, SEC (2011) 876 of 27 October 2011, p. 12). The main beneficiaries of this measure are Germany, the United Kingdom and the Netherlands. Between 2007 and 2013, they have retained 55% of all TOR collection costs (EU-27), or around €18 billion. In 2007, the Council requested the Commission to provide an assessment of the overall administrative costs for member states and the EU of the management, administration and control of the TOR system (see Council, Discharge to be given to the Commission in respect of the implementation of the budget for the financial year 2005, Doc. 5710/07, Brussels, 7 February 2007). Such assessment has not been undertaken yet. It should be observed that a study carried out for the European Parliament has identified structural differences between member states' performances in customs debt recovery (see Administrative performance differences between Member States recovering Traditional Own Resources of the European Union, 28 February 2013, PE 490.668 (www.europarl.europa.eu/RegData/etudes/etudes/join/2013/490668/IPOL-JOIN_ET(2013)490668_EN.pdf).

Note: The impact of these corrections on the UK correction calculation in 2013 is not included.

Source: European Commission, "Financing the EU Budget: Report on the Operation of the Own Resources System", Commission Staff Working Paper, SEC (2011) 876 of 27 October 2011, p. 12.

As shown by Table 4, subject to ratification of the own resources decision by member states, exceptions to the financing arrangements during 2014-2020 will apply in one way or another to a number of member states (11 in 2014).

Table 4. Specific revenue arrangements applicable to some member states (2014-2020)

Member state	Capping of the VAT base to 50% of GNI (2014)	Reduced call rate of the VAT-based resource	Reduced GNI contribution	Rebates	Reduced participation in bearing the cost of the UK rebate
Denmark			x		
Germany		x			x
Croatia	x				
Cyprus	x				
Luxembourg	x				
Malta	x				
Netherlands		x	x		x
Austria			x		x
Slovenia	x				
Sweden		x	x		x
United Kingdom				x	

Source: Author's own elaboration from Council Decision of 26 May 2014 (2014/335/EU, Euratom) on the system of own resources of the European Union, OJ L 168 of 7 June 2014.

Who pays how much?

Expenditure foreseen by the 2014 EU budget amounts to €135.5 billion, or some 6% less compared to the 2013 budget. The own resources needed to finance this expenditure account for 0.99% of the total EU GNI, so well below the ceiling (1.23%) currently in force.

Table 5 below shows the share among member states of national contributions estimated for the 2014 budget.[27] It may be noted that, in general, member states' contributions slightly exceed their share in EU GNI. The United Kingdom represents an exception in this respect. This country contributes significantly less than its share in EU GNI (10.25% against a share in EU GNI of 14.53%).

Table 5. Funding of the EU budget through national contributions (VAT and GNI-based resources) in comparison to GNI (2014 budget, EU-28, €)

Member states	Total 'National contributions' (€)	Share in total 'National contributions' (%)	Share of EU GNI base (%)
(1)	(2)	(3)	(4)
Belgium	3,719,173,706	3.16	2.96
Bulgaria	395,635,841	0.34	0.31
Czech Republic	1,343,409,442	1.14	1.06
Denmark	2,432,887,956	2.07	1.96
Germany	25,060,265,376	21.30	21.07
Estonia	174,498,918	0.15	0.14
Ireland	1,311,068,151	1.11	1.03
Greece	1,655,378,187	1.41	1.34
Spain	9,834,295,817	8.36	7.79
France	20,296,355,175	17.25	16.00
Croatia	419,114,443	0.36	0.33
Italy	14,867,995,428	12.64	11.87
Cyprus	147,770,830	0.13	0.11
Latvia	225,500,402	0.19	0.18

---

[27] It should be noted that own resources estimates for the 2014 budget have been established on the basis of the own resource decision in force (Council Decision 2007/436/EC, Euratom, OJ L 163 of 23 June 2007, p. 17). Some retrospective adjustments in member states burden sharing would be needed once Council Decision of 26 May 2014, op. cit., currently undergoing ratification by member states, will enter into force.

Lithuania	326,724,598	0.28	0.26
Luxembourg	325,642,134	0.28	0.25
Hungary	909,695,924	0.77	0.72
Malta	65,060,424	0.06	0.05
Netherlands	5,507,526,997	4.68	4.65
Austria	2,920,654,659	2.48	2.44
Poland	3,748,526,667	3.19	2.92
Portugal	1,533,546,309	1.30	1.20
Romania	1,377,382,236	1.17	1.12
Slovenia	333,933,232	0.28	0.26
Slovakia	689,553,777	0.59	0.56
Finland	1,955,620,734	1.66	1.53
Sweden	4,011,378,248	3.41	3.37
United Kingdom	12,060,889,112	10.25	14.53
Total	117,649,484,723	100.-	100.-

Source: Author's own elaboration from General budget of the European Union for the financial year 2014 (Tables 5 – column 1 -, and 6 – columns 8 and 9), OJ L 51 of 20 February 2014, pp. I/16 and I/17.

A similar picture is provided when looking at the actual member states' national contributions for the period 2007-2013. Table 6 confirms that in relation to GNI the situation of the United Kingdom is significantly different from that of the other member states. The average weight of this country in the EU GNI is 14.75%, whilst its contribution to the EU budget stands at 10.70%. It should also be noted, however, that to varying degrees Germany, the Netherlands and Sweden have also contributed proportionately less than their share in the EU GNI.

Table 6. Funding of the EU budget through national contributions (VAT and GNI-based resources) in comparison to EU GNI (outturn 2007-2013, EU-27, €)

Member states	'National contributions'(€)	Share in total 'National contributions' (%)	Share of EU GNI (%)
(1)	(2)	(3)	(4)
Belgium	22,949,141,618	3.16	2.88
Bulgaria	2,294,114,649	0.32	0.28
Czech Republic	8,995,310,434	1.24	1.10
Denmark	15,246,376,397	2.10	1.94
Germany	144,350,028,759	19.90	20.72
Estonia	1,001,211,841	0.14	0.12
Ireland	9,204,749,638	1.27	1.13
Greece	14,453,869,327	1.99	1.67
Spain	66,343,188,432	9.15	8.22
France	128,838,672,813	17.76	15.97
Italy	98,474,506,654	13.57	12.38
Cyprus	1,076,839,954	0.15	0.13
Latvia	1,322,859,528	0.18	0.17
Lithuania	1,907,016,535	0.26	0.24
Luxembourg	1,899,610,206	0.26	0.23
Hungary	5,859,788,801	0.81	0.74
Malta	391,808,117	0.05	0.05
Netherlands	27,396,559,320	3.78	4.69
Austria	16,920,847,347	2.33	2.31
Poland	22,249,236,981	3.07	2.73
Portugal	10,812,179,731	1.49	1.31
Romania	8,019,346,367	1.11	1.02
Slovenia	2,302,709,527	0.32	0.28
Slovakia	4,015,883,594	0.55	0.51
Finland	11,994,581,814	1.65	1.48
Sweden	19,464,224,118	2.68	2.96
United Kingdom	77,655,247,244	10.70	14.75
Total	725,439,909,748	100.00	100.00

Source: Author's own elaboration from European Commission, "EU budget 2013 Financial report", Luxembourg, 2014.

Figure 4 below presents the deviation of each member state from the EU-27 average of 'national contributions' in proportion to the GNI, as well as in relation to the population (per capita contribution). The point '0' in the figure represents the EU average, based on cumulative data for the period 2007-2013. EU average values are respectively 0.83% of the EU GNI and €1,453. The analysis shows that for a large majority (23) of EU-27 member states the actual contribution in percentage of GNI was above the EU average. This is the result of the correction mechanisms discussed earlier.

Figure 4. Contribution to EU budget as a % of GNI and per capita (nominal value, €) - Deviation from EU-27 average (outturn 2007-2013)

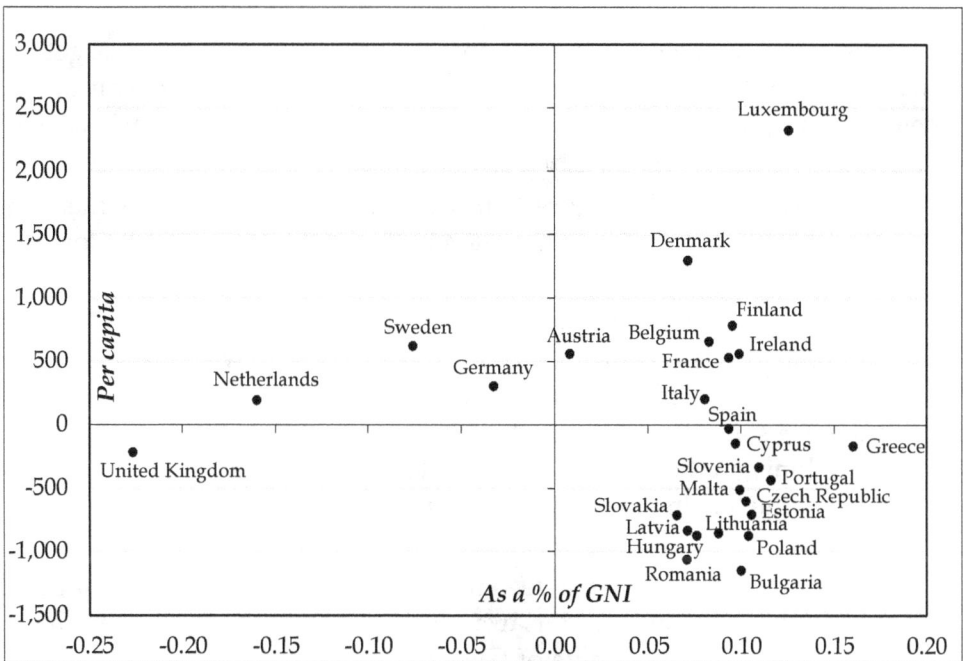

Source: Author's own elaboration from Eurostat data (2010 Population) and European Commission, "2013 Financial Report", Luxembourg, 2014.

More in detail, Figure 4 shows that member states could be divided basically into four categories:

i.   Countries whose contribution is below average for both the GNI ratio and the per capita contribution. The United Kingdom is the only member state in such a situation (0.60% of its GNI and €1,242 of per capita contribution).

ii.   Those whose contribution is below average in terms of GNI ratio but above average in terms of per capita contribution. This is the case of

Germany (0.79% of its GNI and €1,765 of per capita contribution), Sweden (0.75% of its GNI and €2,084 of per capita contribution) and the Netherlands (0.67% of its GNI and €1,653 of per capita contribution).

iii. Those whose contribution is above average for both the GNI ratio and the per capita contribution. Luxembourg, Denmark, Finland, Belgium, Ireland, Austria, France and Italy meet these conditions.

iv. Those whose contribution is above average for the GNI ratio but below average in terms of per capita contribution. This is the case of Spain, Greece and Portugal as well as of the member states having joined the Union after May 2004.

Table 7 compares GNI and national contributions to the EU budget for a number of member states and on a per capita basis. Both values are expressed in purchasing power standard – PPS at market prices. The following conclusions can be drawn on the basis of Table 7:

- As already shown by Figure 4, the United Kingdom is the only member state whose per capita contribution to the EU budget is (far) below the EU-27 average.

- The ratio 'national contributions' per capita (column 6) over GNI per capita (column 2) shows that the share of citizens' wealth allocated to the EU budget is both limited and quite different depending on the member state (see column 8). This share is the lowest in the United Kingdom and the Netherlands. Sweden, Germany and Austria are also below the arithmetical average of the member states considered (5.93%).

- There is no correlation between member states' GNI per capita and the EU budget financing. For example, Denmark and Sweden have practically the same value of GNI-PPS per capita but their per capita contribution to the EU budget is quite different. The same applies to the United Kingdom as compared to Ireland or France.

- When looking at the ranking of countries in relation to the EU-27 average (columns 4 and 5), one can observe that the Netherlands, Sweden and the United Kingdom are far higher in the GNI ranking when compared to their position based on the national contributions paid. The opposite is true for Belgium, Finland, Ireland and France.

Table 7. Average GNI and national contributions (VAT and GNI-based resources) per capita (PPS, outturn 2007-2013, €) – Selected member states

Member state	GNI (PPS) per capita	EU-27 average=100	Member state ranking EU-27 average		Nat'l contri-butions per capita (PPS)	EU-27 average=100	% of (6)/(2)
			GNI	Nat'l contri-butions			
(1)	(2)	(3)	(4)	(5)	(6)	(7)	(8)
Luxembourg	46,967	187.8	1	1	3,133	216.2	6.67
Netherlands	32,257	129.0	2	12	1,507	104.0	4.67
Denmark	31,800	127.1	3	2	2,001	138.1	6.29
Sweden	31,729	126.8	4	9	1,669	115.2	5.26
Austria	31,357	125.4	5	5	1,834	126.6	5.85
Germany	30,371	121.4	6	8	1,690	116.6	5.56
Belgium	29,657	118.6	7	3	1,889	130.4	6.37
Finland	28,886	115.5	8	4	1,866	128.8	6.46
United Kingdom	27,471	109.8	9	13	1,155	79.7	4.21
Ireland	27,450	109.7	10	6	1,780	122.9	6.49
France	27,429	109.7	11	7	1,768	122.0	6.45
Italy	25,271	101.0	12	10	1,606	110.8	6.35
Spain	24,343	97.3	13	11	1,569	108.3	6.45

Note: The conversion in PPS of national contributions has been obtained by applying the ratio GNI in €/GNI in PPS.

Source: Author's own elaboration from Eurostat data (2010 Population; GNI in PPS – Average 2007-2013, 2007-2012 for Ireland, Greece, Luxembourg, Hungary, Poland and Romania) and European Commission, "2013 Financial report", Luxembourg, 2014.

Figure 5 below shows, for the net payer member states, the value of their negative balance in percentage of the GNI. This confirms that this balance represents a rather low share of the GNI, in particular for the United Kingdom.

Figure 5. 'Operating budgetary balances' as a % of GNI – Net-payer member states (outturn 2007-2013)

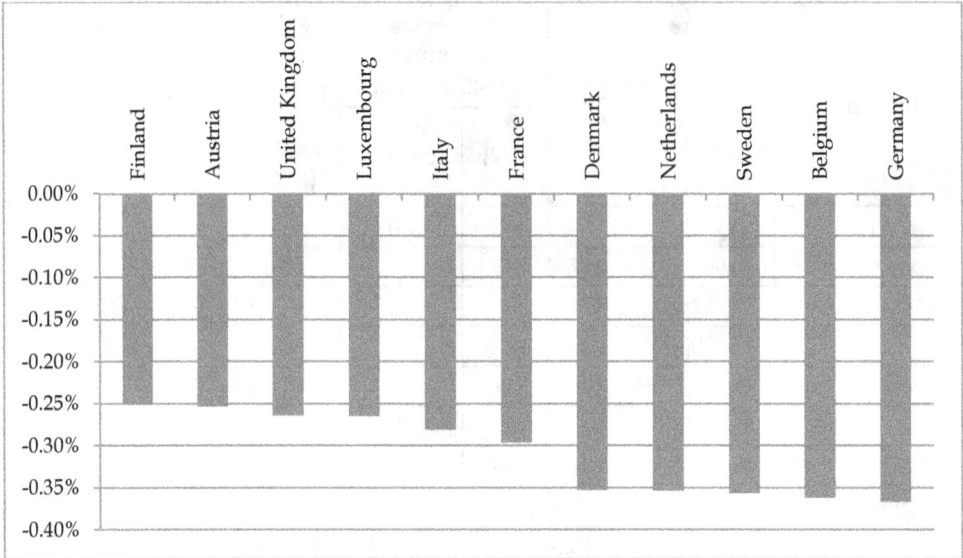

Source: Author's own elaboration based on European Commission, "EU Budget 2013 Financial Report", Luxembourg, 2014.

Concluding remarks

The 'relay' envisaged by the EEC Treaty between national contributions and 'own resources', or between member states' transfers and a direct fiscal levy on citizens making the EU financially independent, has not taken place. EU 'financial autonomy' means no more than member states complying with the obligation they have set for themselves to finance the EU budget each year within the limits of the MFF agreed ceiling. EU revenue arrangements still require approval by national parliaments, despite an elected European Parliament as the institutional place where "[c]itizens are directly represented at Union level".[28]

EU revenue is traditionally a matter restricted to intergovernmental negotiation, whereby revenue and expenditure go hand in hand. This explains that most of EU expenditure is pre-allocated on a geographical basis, as it represents the financial 'return' of national contributions paid to the EU. The rationale of EU revenue arrangements, funded out of the cashbox of the overall taxation, is nothing else than finding for each member

---

[28] See Article 10(2) TEU.

state an acceptable balance between their contributions and EU payments to them. Hence, the number of corrections for several member states to reach the required unanimous agreement. An analysis of these contributions shows that there are significant discrepancies among member states in comparison to a macroeconomic aggregate like GNI or on a per capita basis. Against this background, EU citizens are generally unaware that they contribute to the EU budget and by how much.

The concept of net balances between contributions and EU payments has become the master of the EU financial arrangements. Yet, the conventions that determine these calculations, criticised by the Commission as 'arbitrary' and 'highly questionable' and for encouraging a narrow-sided geographical distribution of EU expenditure, provide only a simplistic view of member states' benefits and their trend. In fact, due to the spillover effects of EU expenditure beyond the borders, member states claiming an imbalance on the basis of 'budgetary balances' calculations may actually appear as net beneficiaries. In this respect, a measure of the impact of EU expenditure in economic terms (increase in the production of goods and services) would show completely different results than 'budgetary balances' calculations.

Given that assessing the benefits of EU expenditure is a legitimate ambition, it would seem appropriate for the Commission to develop alternative and more meaningful methods than 'budgetary balances' calculations. In line with the idea of a budget for 'Europeans' and the consequent need to establish a direct link between citizens and the EU budget, the benefits of EU expenditure should be assessed with reference to EU citizens, and not just to member states. The mid-term review/revision of the MFF to be undertaken by the end of 2016 provides an opportunity to assess the implications of EU expenditure in creating budgetary imbalances. This exercise may also start a discussion on the criteria that could potentially be used to ascertain the existence of a member state's budgetary imbalance.

What is simple is usually not easy.

Jean Monnet

2. SIMPLICITY, TRANSPARENCY, EQUITY AND DEMOCRATIC ACCOUNTABILITY

Following the recent agreement on the 2014-2020 multiannual financial framework, the European Parliament, Council and the European Commission agreed to set up a High-Level Group on Own Resources chaired by former Italian Prime Minister and European Commissioner Mario Monti, to carry out a general review of the own resources system. The High-Level Group will provide a first assessment by the end of 2014. Progress of the work will be examined at the political level in regular meetings, at least once every six months. National Parliaments will be invited to an inter-institutional conference during 2016 to examine the outcome of this work. On this basis, the Commission will assess if new initiatives are appropriate. This assessment will be completed by the end of 2016 at the latest, in parallel with the review of the functioning of the MFF, with a view to possible reforms to be considered for the period covered by the next multiannual financial framework.

Commenting on the first meeting of the High-Level Group in early April 2014, the former EU Budget Commissioner Janusz Lewandowski stated:

> Everybody agrees that the current system is too opaque, too complex and, let's be frank, outdated. However, unanimous agreement on the need to improve the current system is one thing, finding a fairer, more transparent and more modern system likely to be agreed by all is another thing.[29]

---

[29] See "Towards a better, fairer and simpler funding of the EU budget", statement by Commissioner Janusz Lewandowski after the first meeting of the High level Group on Own Resources, 4 April 2014 (http://ec.europa.eu/commission_2010-2014/lewandowski/headlines/index_en.htm?id=201400001200&type=news).

Indeed, the debate about the EU revenue system is an issue dating back to the EEC Rome Treaty of 1957, which opened the prospect of replacing member states' national contributions by 'Community's own resources'.[30] Like the Phoenix, a review of the EU revenue system rises up at regular intervals. The adoption of each MFF since 1988 has been accompanied by a request to review the EU revenue system. So far, all attempts at reform have failed, in particular the introduction of forms of direct EU fiscal revenue.

In fact, not all stakeholders (Parliament, Council or the Commission) share a true motivation for change. The Council's main concern is to avoid any risk of a 'supranational' drift that might eventually lead member states to lose their current tutelage over EU financing arrangements. As shown by the transformation of the VAT-based resource into a national contribution, member states are traditionally reluctant to accept any form of direct fiscal taxation and financial autonomy for the EU. They have already indicated that pursuit of financial autonomy should not undermine equity, transparency, cost-effectiveness and simplicity.[31] And it is certainly no accident that the Council has omitted in the own resource decision applicable to the MFF 2014-2020 to indicate, as proposed by the Commission, that the own resources system "should, as far as possible rely on

---

[30] See Article 201 EEC. As early as 1965, the Commission proposed a global package of measures aimed at establishing a link between financing the CAP, raising independent revenue for the Community and giving wider budgetary powers to the European Parliament. Not only did the Commission envisage a gradual transfer (as of July 1967) of the customs duties and agricultural levies to the EU budget, it also suggested amending Article 201 EEC providing that the Council should consult the European Parliament concerning the replacement of national contributions by 'own resources'. Also, the approval of EU revenue arrangements by national parliaments should have been discontinued once the European Parliament was directly elected (see European Commission, "Financement de la politique agricole commune – Ressources propres de la Communauté – Renforcement des pouvoirs du Parlement européen", COM (65) 150, Brussels, 31 March 1965). It must be remembered that the proposed arrangements for financing agricultural spending were notably at the source of a serious crisis of the Community, the 'empty chair crisis' with France boycotting Council meetings as from July 1965. This crisis was resolved with the Luxembourg compromise (January 1966), providing that "when vital interests of one or more countries are at stake, members of the Council will endeavour to reach solutions that can be adopted by all while respecting their mutual interests".

[31] See European Council, Presidency Conclusions of the Berlin European Council of 24-25 March 1999, point 67.

autonomous own resources in the spirit of the Treaty, rather than on financial contributions from Member States which they widely perceive as national expenditures".[32]

Similarly, the Commission has little reason to feel rushed. There is no fire in the house. The agreed resources are secured from the outset and are paid out without major problems. The best guarantee in this respect is that some 90% of these resources are handed back to member states in the form of EU expenditure.

Only Parliament, which in an initial stage made conditional its approval of the 2014-2020 MFF to a reform of EU revenue, has a real interest in moving forward.[33] Not just as an advocate of EU citizens' interests but, more importantly, in view of possibly extending its prerogatives to the revenue side of the budget, after having obtained with the Treaty of Lisbon a broad co-decision framework for approving the spending programmes and the annual budget, where Parliament is now at an equal level with the Council. In the end, the objective for Parliament could be to establish a parallelism of powers between revenue and expenditure arrangements.

Since any agreement has to be endorsed unanimously by all member states, a confirmation of the status quo remains a serious possibility. The objective 'ally' of such scenario is that the current revenue system allows a stable flow of resources, in line with the MFF agreement. Some may actually consider that the current debate is a kind of distraction or, at most, that redesigning the way the EU gets its revenue is not a top priority.[34]

Indeed, why change a system that has guaranteed a relatively smooth financing of the EU budget?

---

[32] See European Commission, Amended proposal for a Council Decision on the system of own resources of the European Union, Recital No 4, COM (2011) 739, Brussels, 9 November 2011.

[33] See European Parliament Resolutions of 13 June 2012 on the Multiannual Financial Framework and own resources (paragraph 3) and of 23 October 2012 in the interests of achieving a positive outcome of the Multiannual Financial Framework 2014-2020 approval procedure (paragraph 73).

[34] See speech by H. Van Rompuy, "A Curtain went up", 9 November 2010, doc. PCE 256/10

(www.consilium.europa.eu/uedocs/cms_data/docs/pressdata/en/ec/117623.pdf).

Four good reasons for change

The reasons for change have been provided by the MFF 2014-2020 agreement itself, by stating that the general review of the own resources system should be guided by four main criteria: simplicity, transparency, equity and democratic accountability.[35]

More particularly, concerning simplicity, the current system takes advantage of the fact that a revenue collection system is only needed for TOR (Traditional own resources). VAT and GNI-based resources are not 'collected' but just put at the disposal of the EU as financial transfers from national budgets. So, all in all, the current system can be considered as cost-effective if compared to a traditional fiscal collection system. Still, the calculations (and control) for both the VAT and GNI-based resources are complex. Member states' contributions for a given year only become final after several years and are not free from a significant number of difficulties.[36] Moreover, the co-existence of two types of 'national contributions' serves no other purpose than justifying a different burden-sharing among member states. Not least, the calculation of the UK rebate is another complex exercise, which is not exempt from errors.[37]

Nor does the EU revenue system score well in terms of its transparency and democratic accountability. The nature of a transfer from national budgets of most resources and the proliferation over time of ad-hoc corrections for some member states have led to opacity of the system. The famous 'no taxation without representation' principle is applied at EU level the other way round. There is representation (namely through the European

---

[35] See Joint Declaration on Own Resources by Parliament, Council and Commission, Council document 15997/13, ADD 1, point 4, Brussels, 25 November 2013. It should be noted that in its conclusions of 7 and 8 February 2013, the European Council limited these criteria to simplicity, transparency and equity, thus omitting democratic accountability (see European Council Conclusions of 7 and 8 February 2013, doc. EUCO 37/13, Brussels, 8 February 2013, point 111). The same omission can be observed in Recital 3 of Council Decision of 26 May 2014, op. cit.

[36] See footnote 14.

[37] For example, the European Court of Auditors has found that the Commission's calculation of the 2006 definitive amount of this correction resulted in an excessive correction granted to the United Kingdom of €189 million, or 3.5% of the UK rebate for 2006 (see European Court of Auditors, Annual Report concerning the financial year 2010, paragraph 2.16 and annex 2.5, point 7).

Parliament), but no visible and explicit taxation for the EU budget. This makes EU revenue impalpable to the general public, undermining citizens' awareness. Citizens are generally unaware that by paying for example income tax, or any other tax, they may also contribute to financing the EU budget. The European Parliament considers that there is a crucial need for a democratic reform of EU resources because the current system is not subject to parliamentary control at either European or national level, thus violating, in essence, "the letter and spirit of the Treaty".[38]

Since the EU budget is currently designed to be financed by member states (and not directly by citizens), the equity of the system is usually assessed by reference to the GNI, which is traditionally considered the best indicator of a member state's ability to contribute (i.e. proportionality of gross contributions to income across the member states). This explains the current overwhelming weight of the GNI-based resource. According to the Commission, "no own resource can be more equitable". Along the same lines, the European Parliament has indicated that the GNI resource is "equitable in relating contributions to the general level of prosperity of Member States".[39]

Indeed, the rationale of introducing the GNP (later GNI) resource in 1988 was precisely that the more national contributions would be proportional to GNP, the more equity would have been achieved, since the GNP was supposed to measure the prosperity of a country (through its national income) and not, like the GDP, its productive capacity.

However, as shown previously in section 1.5, "Who pays how much?", there is not necessarily a correlation between member states' GNI and their share in the EU budget financing. It is in particular the UK rebate that upsets the correlation with the ability to pay. So, 'horizontal equity', in the sense that the burden should be shared among member states according to an equal ability to contribute, is not fully respected. This undermines the neutrality of the revenue system. The European Parliament has observed

---

[38] See European Parliament, Resolution of 23 October 2012, op. cit., paragraph 71. See also European Parliament, Resolution of 8 June 2011 on Investing in the future: a new Multiannual Financial Framework (MFF) for a competitive, sustainable and inclusive Europe, paragraph 169.

[39] See European Commission, "Financing the European Union", COM (1998) 560, Brussels, 7 October 1998, p. 11 and European Parliament, Resolution of 29 March 2007 on the future of the European Union's own resources, paragraph 23.

that the nature of EU resources and the derogation regimes progressively added have made the EU revenue system "increasingly less equitable and have led to a financing system which has resulted in unacceptable inequalities between Member States".[40]

Concerning 'vertical equity', referring to distribution of income among citizens, a serious threat is represented by the fact that the level of real income is not equal among the member states. Yet, there is no progressivity in contributions to take account of how well off are the citizens of a country or a region compared to the EU average (relative prosperity). In this respect, as shown by Figure 4 and Table 7, the financial burden on a per capita basis is significantly different among EU citizens. One might note, however, that in the EU budget context 'progressivity' is meant to be addressed through 'solidarity', notably by allocating Cohesion funding to less well-off regions.

It should also be observed that the use of GNI for key features of EU revenue (setting of the own resources ceiling, establishment of the GNI-based resource, calculation of the weighted-average rate of the VAT-based resource and capping of its assessment basis) requires that statistical data should not only be reliable and exhaustive, but they should also allow a comparison of 'apples' with 'apples' across member states. The more so as GNI is part of European statistics that underlie important decisions for the economic governance of the EU, in particular to determine European fiscal, macroeconomic and monetary policies. Therefore, GNI also plays a role in building citizens' trust in European statistics.[41]

As the chief provider of European statistics, Eurostat has the challenging role of ensuring that the "production of Union statistics shall conform to impartiality, reliability, objectivity, scientific independence, cost-effectiveness and statistical confidentiality" (see Article 338(2) TFEU). The number of pending (and sometimes longstanding) issues related to member states' GNI calculations shows that national statistical processes may not always guarantee that economic activities are estimated in accordance with the European System of Accounts.[42] Despite all efforts to ensure the best

---

[40] See European Parliament, Resolution of 8 June 2005 on Policy Challenges and Budgetary Means of the Enlarged Union 2007–2013, paragraph L.

[41] It should be noted that Europeans' opinions on the trustworthiness of the official statistics are split, with a slight majority tending not to trust them. See Special Eurobarometer 323, "Europeans' knowledge of economic indicators", January 2010, p. 44 (http://ec.europa.eu/public_opinion/archives/ebs/ebs_323_en.pdf).

[42] See footnote 14.

accuracy possible, GNI remains by its own nature an aggregation of estimates, based on concepts, methods and sources of data whose harmonisation in practice cannot be absolute. In this respect, one key issue is the reliability and comparability across countries of the estimate of the 'underground economy'. Since, by definition, the latter cannot be measured directly, an adequate assessment of this estimate would require full transparency on the methods and sources used by the statistical offices. Yet, this is not available in all EU countries.

The European Court of Auditors has observed that considerable efforts have been made since 2005 to enhance the European statistical system. However, the move towards a better quality framework for European statistics is slow, is yet incomplete and remains a challenge for all those involved. The European Statistics Code of Practice sets demanding standards, but it has only been partly implemented and lacks strong verification and enforcement tools. The Court also reported weaknesses concerning Eurostat's risk assessment relating to member states' compilation of national accounts, the application of a consistent approach when carrying out its verification procedures in the member states, the performance of sufficient work at that level and adequate reporting thereupon.[43]

The drawbacks of the 2011 Commission's proposals

According to the Commission, the current EU revenue system "performs poorly with regard to most assessment criteria". It "is opaque and complex. This limits democratic oversight of the system". It is "almost impossible for EU citizens to ascertain who effectively bears the cost of financing the EU". Many member states "perceive the system to be unfair. More importantly perhaps, the way the EU budget is financed creates a tension which poisons every debate about the EU budget". This "contributes to an increasing focus Member States place on a narrow 'accounting' approach with the main objective of maximising financial returns from the EU budget". In short, "EU financing has primarily been treated as an accounting mechanism with two

---

[43] See European Court of Auditors, Special Report No. 12/2012, "Did the Commission and Eurostat improve the process for producing reliable and credible European statistics?" Luxembourg, 2012, pp. 107-108 and Special Report No. 11/2013, "Getting the Gross National Income (GNI) data right: A more structured and better-focused approach would improve the effectiveness of the Commission's verification", Luxembourg, 2013, pp. 95-97.

main objectives: ensuring sufficient financing of EU expenditures and incorporating the increasing number of correcting mechanisms". Finally, with the exception of customs duties, "the EU resources currently display almost no link to – nor do they support – EU policy objectives".[44]

Against this background, the Commission has put forward, alongside its proposal of MFF 2014-2020, a reform of the own resources system in view of its introduction on 1 January 2014.[45] This reform, which was eventually not adopted by the Council, had three main objectives: i) the simplification of member states' contributions, ii) the introduction of new own resources and iii) the reduction of existing contributions from member states.

The objective of simplification was principally sought through two main measures:

- First, the abolition of the current VAT-based own resource, which is considered complex and requiring much administrative work to arrive at a harmonised base; it is also a source of the opacity of member states' contributions to the budget while offering little or no added value compared to the GNI-based own resource.

- Secondly, the introduction of lump-sum reductions in the GNI-based resource payments to replace the sometimes complex correction mechanisms (above all, the UK rebate) dealing with the budgetary burdens that some member states consider excessive when compared to their relative prosperity.

As a consequence of the incorporation of all corrections into lump sums, the Commission also proposed to reduce the TOR collection costs retained by the member states from 25% to 10%.

The proposal of introducing new own resources has been based on the assessment of six potential candidates and their variants (financial sector taxation; revenue from auctioning under the EU Emissions Trading System; taxation of the aviation sector; an EU VAT; an EU energy tax and an EU corporate income tax). The Commission concluded in favour of a new VAT own resource and a resource based on a financial transaction tax (FTT) in view of reducing member states' contributions to the EU budget.

---

[44] See European Commission, SEC (2011) 876 of 27 October 2011, op. cit., p. 3, 4 and 19.

[45] See European Commission, Proposal for a Council Decision on the system of own resources of the European Union, COM (2011) 510, Brussels, 29 June 2011.

As shown in Table 8, by 2020 some 40% of the EU budget would have been financed by the FTT and VAT-based resources. A similar amount would have been provided by the GNI-based resource, hence meeting Parliament's request to reduce the share of GNI-based contributions to a maximum of 40%, and the balance by TOR resources.[46]

Table 8. Estimated evolution of the structure of EU financing (2012-2020)

	Draft budget 2012		2020	
	€ billion	% of own resources	€ billion	% of own resources
Traditional own resources	19.3	14.7	30.7	18.9
Existing national contributions, of which:	111.8	85.3	65.6	40.3
VAT-based own resource	14.5	11.1	-	-
GNI-based own resource	97.3	74.2	65.6	40.3
New own resources of which:	-	-	66.3	40.8
New VAT resource	-	-	29.4	18.1
EU financial transaction tax	-	-	37.0	22.7
Total own resources	**131.1**	**100.0**	**162.7**	**100.0**

Source: European Commission, Proposal for a Council Decision on the system of own resources of the European Union, COM (2011) 510, Brussels, 29 June 2011, p. 5.

New VAT-based resource

The Commission has explored two options for a new VAT-based resource: a parallel system to that operating in the member states and a revenue transfer mechanism. The first option has been discarded because the Commission thought that a VAT-based resource alongside member states' VAT would have led in practice to the creation of a double VAT system. The Commission opted therefore for the simplest solution, considered equivalent in terms of revenue but with limited impact on businesses and less impact on national tax administrations.

---

[46] See, for example, European Parliament, Resolution of 3 July 2013 on the political agreement on the Multiannual Financial Framework 2014-2020, paragraph 13.

The VAT-based resource would have derived from the application of a single EU rate (maximum 2%) on the net value of supplies of goods and services, intra-EU acquisitions of goods and the importation of goods that are subject to the standard VAT rate in every member state. This means that a standard-rated supply in a member state would have been subject to the VAT own resource unless the same supply was subject to a reduced rate or an exemption in another member state. Thus, the tax base would have corresponded to the smallest common denominator of national VAT systems.

In practice, the VAT-based resource would have required:

- The Commission to calculate (on the basis of national accounts data, consumption data or other sources) a single EU-wide average proportion of VAT receipts from common standard-rated transactions in every member state; and

- Each member state to apply this proportion to its total VAT receipts. Then it would have used its own standard rate to obtain its chargeable base, and applied the call rate for own resources to the chargeable base to determine the EU budget revenue. Unlike the existing VAT-based resource, the revenue stream would not have been capped in percentage of the GNI.

The Commission's proposal raises a number of critical issues:

- The proposed new VAT-based resource beats a retreat from a previous proposition made in 2004 (and confirmed in 2010), which aimed at introducing a VAT-based resource through an EU VAT rate, incorporated in and levied together with the national rate, and thus on the same taxable base.[47] The EU VAT rate would have created a visible and direct link with the citizen. At the same time, citizens would not have supported an additional tax burden as the EU VAT rate would have been offset by an equivalent decrease of the national VAT rate. Member states would have transferred to the EU budget the same percentage of each national VAT base. Despite the fact that this proposal would have met Parliament's longstanding request for a genuine VAT own resource, the Commission did not table any concrete legislative proposal in this respect.

---

[47] See European Commission, "Financing the European Union", Vol. I, COM (2004) 505 final, p. 11 and Vol. II, p. 53, Brussels, 14 July 2004; "The EU Budget review", Technical annexes, SEC (2010) 7000, Brussels, 19 October 2010, p. 34.

- Since it would have been levied on member states and not on citizens, the new VAT-based resource did not seek to provide a solution to the opacity of the EU financing system. Due to the absence of an explicit link with the taxpayer, this resource would have continued to be perceived as a national expenditure.

- If some simplification would have been introduced compared to the current arrangements, the new VAT-based resource would have required the establishment of an EU-wide 'common' basket of standard-rated goods and services. On this basis, the Commission would have determined a single EU-wide average proportion of VAT receipts from standard-rated transactions in every member state. This one-off calculation for the whole period 2014-2020 would have been based on the same type of complex statistical data used for the calculation of the current VAT-based resource.[48] Thus, the accuracy of this calculation would have been of the outmost importance and would have depended on the availability of uniform or equivalent sources and statistical methods. Moreover, the 'common' basket mentioned above should have been monitored on a regular basis to ensure its continued relevance due to the variation over time of the scope of the rates in the different member states. The fact that the Commission did not reveal the member states' share within its overall estimate (see Table 8 above), seems to confirm that this calculation may not have represented a straightforward process.

Financial transaction tax

The significant amount of public funds expended to bail out the financial sector during the global economic crisis has triggered a broad demand, advocated in particular by the European Parliament, for a 'Robin Hood' tax to correct for the current under-taxation in that sector, to contribute to the costs of dealing with the crisis and reduce public deficits.[49]

---

[48] See European Court of Auditors, Opinion No 2/2012 of 20 March 2012, point 17.

[49] See for example European Parliament Resolutions of 8 June 2011, op. cit., of 23 May 2012 on the proposal for a Council directive on a common system of financial transaction tax and amending Directive 2008/7/EC; of 21 May 2013 on the Annual Tax Report: how to free the EU potential for economic growth; of 3 July 2013 on the proposal for a Council directive implementing enhanced cooperation in the area of financial transaction tax. The Commission has indicated that EU member states have

This development has prompted the Commission to consider forms of taxation for the financial sector and to envisage using part of the resulting revenue to finance the EU budget. The Commission analysed two basic options: a financial transaction tax (FTT) and a financial activities tax (FAT) as proposed by the IMF's Report to the G-20.[50] It concluded that an FTT was the preferred option, taking into account its revenue potential and its impact on excessive specific risk-taking. Thus, the Commission adopted in September 2011 a proposal for a Council Directive on an EU FTT common system whose main objectives were:

- To tackle fragmentation of the Single Market that an uncoordinated patchwork of national financial transaction taxes would create;

- To ensure that the financial sector makes a fair and substantial contribution to public finances with a view to cover the cost of the crisis and also to reduce member states' contributions to the EU budget; and

- To create, through a kind of 'polluter-pays' principle, appropriate disincentives for financial transactions that do not contribute to the efficiency of financial markets or to the real economy.[51]

According to the Commission, an FTT collected at EU level would constitute a first step towards its application at global level. At the same time, the allocation of part of its revenue to the EU budget would provide new sources of revenue whilst reducing member states' *juste retour* claims.

The suggested introduction of an FTT has generated from the outset a significant discussion on the realism of its alleged benefits and on the risk of delocalisation of financial services in the absence of a general application

---

committed €4.6 trillion to bail out the financial sector during the financial crisis whilst this sector enjoys a tax advantage of approximately €18 billion per year because of the VAT exemption on financial services (see European Commission, Press release IP/11/1085 of 28 September 2011). The reason for VAT exemption of most financial services is that the major part of financial services' income is margin-based and therefore is not easily taxable under the current VAT arrangements.

[50] See M. Keen., R. Krelove and J. Norregaard, "The Financial Activities Tax", in S. Claessens, M. Keen and C. Pazarbasioglu (eds), *Financial Sector Taxation, The IMF's Report to the G-20 and Background Material*, International Monetary Fund, Washington, D.C., September 2010, p. 118.

[51] See European Commission, Proposal for a Council Directive on a common system of financial transaction tax and amending Directive 2008/7/EC, COM (2011) 594, Brussels, 28 September 2011.

outside the FTT area. For example, Parliament remarked that the "FTT will truly achieve its objectives only if it is introduced at global level".[52]

Obviously, the debate on the introduction of an FTT reflected the significant interests at stake, not just of the financial sector but also at the level of the member states. In this respect, it appeared clear by mid-2012 that the Commission's proposal for introducing an FTT harmonised at EU level was unlikely to receive the required member states' unanimous support in the foreseeable future. Therefore, on the basis of the request of 11 member states (Belgium, Germany, Estonia, Greece, Spain, France, Italy, Austria, Portugal, Slovenia and Slovakia), the Commission submitted a proposal for enhanced cooperation in the area of a financial transaction tax. The proposal was endorsed by the Council in early 2013.[53]

To prevent driving taxable financial transactions outside the 11 participating member states, the FTT proposed by the Commission would apply on the basis of the principle of the country of residence of the financial institution, supplemented by the country of issuance principle. Thus, financial transactions would be taxed, regardless of where the transaction takes place in the world. The FTT would not concern transactions involving

---

[52] See European Parliament, Resolution of 3 July 2013, op. cit. For a review of pro and contra arguments, see PricewaterhouseCoopers LLP, "Financial transaction tax: The impact and arguments", November 2013 (www.abi.org.uk/~/media/Files/Documents/Publications/Public/2013/Taxatio n/Financial%20Transaction%20Tax%20Literature%20Review.ashx).

[53] Enhanced cooperation (see Article 20 TEU and Articles 326 to 334 TFEU) aims to overcome a situation whereby it proves difficult to reach unanimous agreement among member states, thus allowing those wanting to move ahead with a common approach to do so. A minimum of nine member states are needed for enhanced cooperation to be allowed. Shortly after the Council approval, the United Kingdom lodged an action in the European Court of Justice against the Council Decision, on the ground that it is contrary to Article 327 TFEU because it authorises the adoption of an FTT with extraterritorial effects which will fail to respect the competences, rights and obligations of the non-participating states (see Case law C-209/13, United Kingdom of Great Britain and Northern Ireland v Council of the European Union). In its ruling of 30 April 2014, the European Court of Justice confirmed the legality of the enhanced cooperation and rejected as premature and speculative the United Kingdom's arguments on the impact of the FTT on non-participating member states, since the tax has not yet been adopted. One may expect that the contention will emerge again once the implementing measures will be ultimately adopted by the participating member states.

private households or small and medium enterprises (SMEs) such as house mortgages, bank borrowings by SMEs or insurance contracts. Currency exchange transactions and the raising of capital by enterprises or public bodies would not be taxed either. The proposed taxation minimum rates are at 0.1% for shares and bonds, units of collective investment funds, money market instruments, repurchase agreements and securities lending agreements, and 0.01% for derivative products. Participating member states would be free to apply higher rates.[54]

The main taxpayers should be the financial institutions operating financial transactions and actually around 85% of the transactions take place purely between them. However, as any tax has in the end to be paid by somebody, financial institutions would most likely pass on the cost to their clients. The FTT will thus have a progressive distributional implication, putting the burden on richer individuals.

Whether and to what extent, final payers will be made aware that a part of the tax might accrue to the EU budget remains an open question. Initially, it was envisaged that the FTT would be collected by economic operators rather than by the member states. Indeed, given the relative limited number of centres of taxation, it would have been possible to set up a relatively straightforward collection system managed at EU level and, hence, a direct source of financing for the EU budget. This option has been superseded by the proposed FTT Directive providing that member states' administrations will be responsible for collecting the tax.

The intention of participating countries is to work on a progressive implementation of the FTT, focusing initially on the taxation of shares and some derivatives. The objective is still to reach an agreement on this first stage before the end of 2014. Three issues lie at the heart of the discussions: the scope of application of the tax (which shares and derivatives); whether it will use the principle of country of residence of the financial institution or of the country of issuance; the arrangements for the payment of the tax and how the income generated is to be shared out.

According to the Commission's revenues projections, the FTT applied under enhanced cooperation would generate, depending on market reactions, between €30 and €35 billion a year (of which more than one-third

---

[54] See European Commission, Proposal for a Council Directive implementing enhanced cooperation in the area of financial transaction tax, Brussels, COM (2013) 71, Brussels, 14 February 2013. See also the Press release MEMO/13/98 of 14 February 2013.

would come from securities and the rest from derivatives), so slightly more than half of what could have been expected for an implementation in all member states. These projections (see Figure 6) are based on the share of each participating member state in total FTT revenues, with reference to the size of their underlying economies. On this basis, the amounts could range from €95 million for Estonia to €11.75 billion for Germany.

Figure 6. Breakdown of revenues according to GDP in PPS (2011) in member states participating in enhanced cooperation on FTT

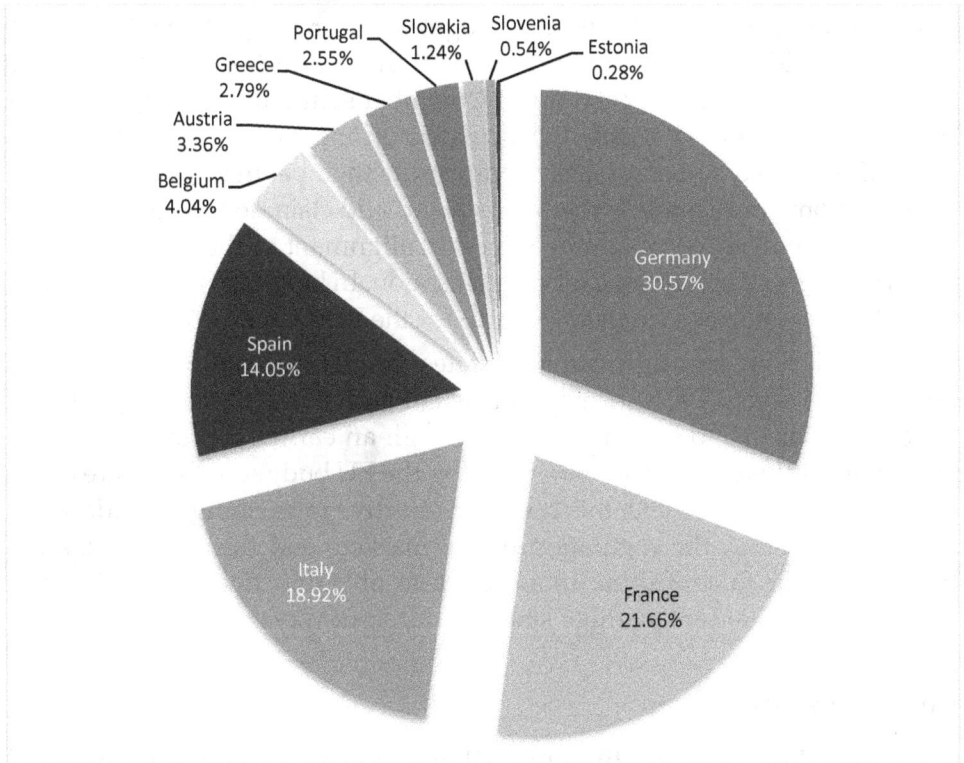

Source: European Commission, "Impact assessment of the proposed Directive implementing enhanced cooperation in the area of financial transaction tax", SWD (2013) 28, 14 February 2013, p. 24.

According to the Commission's estimates, an FTT applied at EU level could have provided to the EU budget by 2020 an amount of €37 billion a year, which would fund around 23% of its expenditure (see Table 8). With the application of the FTT to 11 member states, a proportional reduction would leave available for the EU budget around €21 billion a year, or 13% of the revenue needs estimated. However, due in particular to the risk of delocalisation mentioned above and the intrinsic variations of the underlying economic context, the actual amount of FTT revenue is rather unpredictable. Such instability would likewise create tensions at the level of the balancing resource, the GNI-based resource. The above shows that in the current circumstances, the FTT does not fulfil one key criteria to become an own resource, namely the maturity and stability of its assessment basis.

Furthermore, the European Council made clear that the enhanced cooperation on the FTT would not affect non-participating member states and the calculation of the UK rebate.[55] This means that while the overall resources to be allocated to the EU budget will remain unchanged, the FTT revenue would reduce by the same amount the volume of the GNI resource for the 11 member states. Yet, for these member states, the reduction of their payments for the GNI resource (calculated on the basis of the ratio in the total EU GNI) may not necessarily compensate their payments out of the FTT revenue. Some participating member states could claim to face an imbalance and therefore insist on obtaining either an alignment of their GNI and FTT contributions or another form of compensation. In both cases the *raison d'être* of the FTT revenue as a financing source for the EU budget would disappear.

Finally, as several member states are strongly opposed to the introduction of an FTT, it seems inconsistent with the idea of a budget for all European citizens, to fund part of it through an earmarked tax applied by only some of them. In any event, financing the EU budget with a share of the FTT revenue will not make this tax more effective in reaching its underlying objectives. Indeed, the regulation of the markets and the wish to ask the financial sector to contribute to a reduction of public deficits can be (and actually is) pursued by member states in different ways.

Correction mechanism

As discussed above, one of the aims of the Commission's proposals to amend the own resources system was the progressive phasing-out of all correction mechanisms. In this respect, the Commission recalled the principles set at the 1984 Fontainebleau European Council (and reiterated by the 1999 Berlin European Council), indicating that expenditure policy is ultimately the essential means of resolving the question of budgetary imbalances and that any member state sustaining a budgetary burden that is excessive in relation

---

[55] See European Council conclusions of 7-8 February 2013, document EUCO 37-13, op. cit., point 115.

to its relative prosperity may benefit from a correction at the appropriate time. The Commission clarified in particular that a correction mechanism "should be closely related to the expenditure policy enshrined in the multiannual financial framework"; it should reflect "the important developments in the financing of the Union" and take account of the levels of prosperity of the member states concerned.[56] The Commission also pointed out: "In the context of a reform of EU financing, any new correction mechanism will need to be carefully justified, not only by way of debatable accounting measurements (...), but in view of the overall balance of benefits brought by the EU budget and policies, and reflect the relative prosperity of the Member States concerned."[57] The Commission finally elaborated some guiding principles for defining and assessing possible correction mechanisms for the future: 'Fairness', 'Transparency and Simplicity', 'Limited in time' and 'No negative impact on incentives to implement EU budget'.[58]

The Commission started its analysis from an assessment of the justification of the current UK rebate. Similarly to prior reviews made in 1998 and 2004, the Commission concluded that the context at the basis of the creation of the UK rebate in 1984 (low UK share in EU agricultural expenditure on which the EU budget was concentrated; and high share of the UK VAT base in relation to its GNP) had evolved fundamentally.[59] Most importantly, being based on a conventional ceiling on the United Kingdom's budgetary balance, the rebate takes no account of the evolution of the relative wealth of a country that was one of the poorest member states at accession but has become since then one of the richest. Despite a change in

---

[56] See European Commission, COM (2011) 739 of 9 November 2011, op. cit., Recitals No 11 and 12.

[57] See European Commission, SEC (2011) 876 of 27 October 2011, op. cit., p. 44.

[58] See European Commission, SEC (2011) 876 of 27 October 2011, op. cit., pp. 46-47. The principle 'No negative impact on incentives to implement EU budget' refers to the fact that the current UK rebate, based on net balances, reduces the incentive for the country to spend money allocated to it in the context of EU policies: two-thirds of EU payments are cancelled out by a reduction of the UK rebate.

[59] For the 1998 analysis, see European Commission, COM (1998) 560 of 7 October 1998, op. cit., p. 20 and Annex IV; for the 2004 analysis, see European Commission, COM (2004) 505 final of 14 July 2004, Vol. II, op. cit., p. 18; for the 2011 analysis, see European Commission, COM (2011) 510 of 29 June 2011, op. cit., pp. 5-8 and SEC (2011) 876 of 27 October 2011, op. cit., part III, p. 41.

the rebate's arrangements to avoid an inflation of its amount due to the additional enlargement-related expenditure after 2004, the size of the UK rebate remains at a significant level and with an upward trend (see Figure 3).

Hence, to address a difference of treatment with other major net contributors, the Commission proposed replacing all existing correction mechanisms with a system of lump-sum reductions on GNI-based resource payments. In particular, for the period 2014–2020, a gross reduction in annual GNI contributions should have been granted to Germany, the Netherlands, Sweden and the United Kingdom for an overall amount of €7.5 billion (€4.333 billion net).[60]

At first sight, a lump-sum system meets the criteria of simplicity and creates no particular disincentives in implementing EU policies. When assessing the Commission's proposal against the criteria of 'transparency', one should note that the decision on which member states should benefit from a lump-sum correction has been based on a net balance indicator and an analysis of the ratio of that balance to relative prosperity. Then, the corrections were calibrated so that the four member states mentioned above arrive at a comparable ratio. However, while acknowledging that a "correction should be transparent and easy to understand", and that lump-sum reduction on GNI payments would apply strictly to those member states "for which a perceived excessive budgetary burden can be demonstrated",[61] the Commission did not make explicit the criteria used to

---

[60] See European Commission, COM (2011) 510 of 29 June 2011, op. cit., p. 7 and p. 17. According to data provided by the Commission to the European Court of Auditors, the gross and net reductions in GNI contributions would have been as follows: Germany €2.5 billion gross and €0.99 billion net; the Netherlands €1.05 billion gross and €0.683 billion net; Sweden €0.35 billion gross and €0.119 billion net; the United Kingdom €3.6 billion gross and €2.542 billion net (see European Court of Auditors, Opinion No 2/2012 of 20 March 2012, op. cit., point 39). In theory, the difference between 'gross' and 'net' is explained by the fact that, unlike for the current UK rebate, also member states benefitting for such corrections would participate in their financing. However, in the absence of the underlying calculation, it is not possible to explain why this difference is of -29% for the United Kingdom while for the Netherlands, Germany and Sweden the difference is respectively –35%, –60% and –66%.

[61] See European Commission, COM (2011) 739 of 9 November 2011, op. cit., Recital No 11, and SEC (2011) 876 of 27 October 2011, op. cit., p. 47.

define when the budgetary burden of a member state can be considered excessive and it has not unveiled the details of its calculations, including to the Court of Auditors.[62] Also, the Commission did not foresee a mechanism for monitoring, over time, whether a budgetary burden continues to be excessive and whether other member states would qualify for a correction.

In particular, there is no indication that the Commission has reached its conclusion on which member states should be granted a correction on the basis of an assessment "of the overall balance of benefits brought by the EU budget and policies".[63] Most likely, this conclusion has been drawn from the usual net-balance calculations, on the basis of an estimated allocation of expenditure of the 2014-2020 MFF. Yet, as underlined by the Commission itself, such calculations are merely an accounting exercise of certain financial costs and benefits, based on 'arbitrary' and 'highly questionable' conventions.

Without access to the methodology used and the underlying data, an evaluation of the 'fairness' of the Commission's proposal is hardly possible. This is particularly the case for understanding on what basis, despite high levels of prosperity achieved by the four member states mentioned above, only them and no other net-payer countries can justify a budgetary burden that might be considered excessive when compared to their relative prosperity. For example, in the period 2007-2013 (see Table 6), Germany, the Netherlands, Sweden and the United Kingdom have contributed proportionally less than their share in the GNI. The opposite is true for France and (notably) Italy, which, as shown in Table 7 (column 3), have recorded a lower relative prosperity during 2007-2013 (measured in GNI-PPS per capita) than Germany, the Netherlands, Sweden and the United Kingdom. At the same time (see column 6), France's contribution (per capita) is higher than that of all latter member states; and Italy's contribution (per capita) is higher than that of the Netherlands.

Furthermore, it could have been useful to consider the anticipated 'operating budgetary balances' ratio in relation to GNI for the period 2014-2020. This is because, compared to the 2007-2013 period, one should note not only an overall reduction of funds (almost -4%) but also significant changes in the Headings. This is notably the case for 'Competitiveness for growth and jobs' (+37%); 'Economic, social and territorial cohesion' (-8%);

---

[62] See European Court of Auditors, Opinion No 2/2012 of 20 March 2012, op. cit., point 43.

[63] See European Commission, SEC (2011) 876 of 27 October 2011, op. cit., p. 44.

'Sustainable Growth: Natural Resources' (-11%) and 'Security and citizenship' (+27%). In the absence of the anticipated 'operating budgetary balances' ratio for the period 2014-2020, the best proxy available is the ratio based on the outturn 2017-2013 (see Figure 5). One may see that the negative balance ratio of Belgium and Denmark, for which the Commission has not proposed a correction in the current period, is higher or comparable to that of Germany, the Netherlands, Sweden and the United Kingdom (whose negative balance is the lowest after Finland and Austria). Finally, only Belgium, Sweden and Germany (with respectively, -0.36%, -0.36% and -037% of their GNI) have exceeded the threshold set by the Commission in 2004 as the maximum accepted level of financial solidarity (-035% of a member state's GNI), beyond which a correction was deemed justified.[64] Still, the rationale of this threshold is purely conventional and, as discussed above, the differences in the pattern of expenditure in the 2014-2020 period may well have an impact in the ultimate destination of EU funds.

Due to the difficulties mentioned above, it is not possible for parliaments and indeed for EU citizens (who will be ultimately affected by the resulting burden-sharing) to exert a proper scrutiny of the Commission's proposal, in line with the principles of transparency and openness set in the Treaties.[65]

This absence of transparency adds opacity to a system already criticised for its opaqueness. It generates mistrust among member states and it therefore provides an objective ground for keeping the status quo. Indeed,

---

[64] The Commission proposed in 2004 to introduce a generalised correction mechanism, as a sort of safety net for large net-payers whose contributions (calculated on the basis of the net budgetary balance) exceeded 0.35% of a member state's GNI. Net positions exceeding such a threshold would have been eligible for a correction (at a rate of 66%). The maximum refund volume was limited to €7.5 billion a year, financed by all member states based on their relative share of GNI (see European Commission, COM (2004) 505 final of 14 July 2004, Vol. II, op. cit., p. 41). The Commission's proposal was eventually not adopted. It should be noted that a number of correction mechanisms have been envisaged over the years (for a review, see Heinemann et al., 2008, p. 110). Although using different definitions of 'budgetary balances', all these mechanisms are based on a balance of member states' contributions to and payments from the EU budget. Therefore, they face the same conceptual weaknesses as the Commission's calculations, as discussed in the section 'To each its own'.

[65] See Articles 1 TEU, 10 TEU, 13(1) TEU and 15 TFEU.

neither the current UK rebate nor the related abatements on this rebate granted to Germany, the Netherlands, Austria and Sweden have expiration dates, since they are part of the own resources decision, which remains applicable until a new one is (unanimously) adopted. These abatements are therefore 'ironclad'. This shows that the UK rebate lies at the crossroad of any reform of the EU financing system.

Finally, concerning the proposed limitation in time of the lump sums, linking corrections to the MFF duration would only provide an apparent progress. This is because a limitation in time will not represent by itself a guarantee against perpetuation of such corrections, as shown by the outcome of the 2014-2020 MFF negotiation.[66] Once granted, a reduction in the contributions to the EU budget tends to be considered by the beneficiary member states as an *acquis*.

Reducing the burden on national budgets?

One of the key aims pursued by the 2011 Commission's proposals for reforming the revenue system was to relieve the current burden on national Treasuries to finance the EU budget. This objective was linked in particular to the introduction of the FTT, whose revenue should have reduced national contributions by an equal amount. Yet, there is no 'magic' in this initiative as the FTT will in principle increase overall taxation, although by putting its burden on richer individuals. Regardless of whether or not a share of the FTT revenue will finance the EU budget, member states will still have to provide the same amount of resources to fund the EU budget. Hence, the impact of funding the EU budget through the FTT would be limited to a different distribution among national fiscal resources in backing the own resources payments; no more than a clearing entry in national accounts.

Still, reducing the burden on public budgets, notably in times of financial constraints, is a legitimate objective. A first main direction to progress towards this objective is through the rationalisation of expenditure, in particular with the aim of looking at the EU and the national budgets as integrated instruments of public policies. As noted by Parliament, since the

---

[66] For example, the 2007-2013 MFF provided for differentiated call-up rates for the VAT-based contribution and gross reductions of the GNI contributions for some member states. The 2014-2020 MFF continues to provide similar forms of compensation for those countries. See the section 'EU revenue: A short history'.

volume of the EU budget is very limited compared to national budgets, there is a need to create synergies between these budgets in order to implement common EU strategies, giving greater impact to European policies.[67] The idea is that less funds from the EU budget do not necessarily mean less public funds for a given policy, but rather the choice for a different level of government, also in view of the specific needs of each of the member states.

The awareness of this issue is witnessed by a declaration of the European Parliament, the Council and the Commission that agreed, in view of the preparation for the post-2020 multiannual financial framework, "to work together with the objective of cost savings and better synergies at national and European levels in order to improve the effectiveness of public spending in matters subject to the EU's action".[68] The mid-term review/revision of the MFF to be undertaken by the end of 2016 actually provides a first opportunity in this respect.

One area deserving particular attention seems to be research spending for which the Treaty already provides (Article 181(1) TFEU) that "The Union and the Member States shall coordinate their research and technological development activities so as to ensure that national policies and Union policy are mutually consistent". Putting in place the European Research Area (ERA) as a unified research platform will require greater collaboration from the EU and national levels, within individual countries and also at EU level where the Research and Cohesion programmes provide the most significant funding opportunities. As indicated by the Commission, "Europe needs critical mass to efficiently address grand challenges and to make the best use of available resources in Europe".[69] The significant number of actors, levels and objectives pursued makes the duplication of efforts a significant risk. Addressing such risk through a more strategic alignment of the various research programmes might save resources and, most importantly, avoid an

---

[67] See European Parliament, Resolution of 15 June 2010 on the mandate for the trilogue on the 2011 draft budget, paragraph 15.

[68] See Joint Declaration by Parliament, Council and Commission on improving effectiveness of public spending in matters subject to EU's action, Council document 15997/13, ADD 1, Brussels, 25 November 2013.

[69] See European Commission, "European Research area progress report 2013", COM (2013) 637, Brussels, 20 September 2013, p. 4. As pointed out by Núñez Ferrer & Katarivas (2014:1), while the EU R&D share of expenditure as a percentage of the total is only 5%, the fact that this funding excludes many capital expenditures that member states cover (e.g. buildings, existing machinery, non-R&D linked staff) means that EU funding is essential in some EU priority areas of research.

indiscriminate fiscal consolidation at the expense of R&D, which could potentially threaten the chances for increasing economic growth and job creation in the future.

Yet, a main avenue for reducing the burden on public budgets is to ensure that all revenue that should accrue to them is actually collected. In this respect, in the framework of a wider reform initiated by its Green Paper on the future of VAT, the Commission has identified in the VAT area a potential to generate new revenue streams, for both national budgets and the EU budget:

> Broadening the tax base, reducing the scope for fraud, improving the administration of the tax and reducing compliance costs in the context of a broad reform of VAT, could deliver important results and generate new revenue streams for the Member States. A fraction of the gains derived from this initiative could be attributed to the EU level, and these could be further increased as the VAT system improved its performance.[70]

It is a fact that member states' VAT losses are significant.[71] The magnitude of uncollected VAT revenue represents a 'litmus test' of a country's ability to manage the tax effectively, in particular of the strength of its management system in terms of its day-to-day supervision (for example, the possibility of performing a sufficient number of far-reaching controls involving often complex relations between various operators) and of the legislative framework in which it operates (fraud opportunities offered by regulatory loopholes).

---

[70] See European Commission, SEC (2011) 876 of 27 October 2011, op. cit., p. 5. For the Green Paper on the future of VAT, see European Commission, "Towards a simpler, more robust and efficient VAT system", COM (2010) 695, Brussels, 1 December 2010.

[71] A conventional way to establish a proxy of VAT losses consists in calculating the 'VAT gap', i.e. the difference between the expected VAT revenue and VAT actually collected. It is commonly thought that VAT fraud is an important contributor to this revenue shortfall. An estimated €177 billion in VAT revenues was lost due to non-compliance or non-collection in 2012 (€171 billion in 2011), according to the latest VAT gap study published by the Commission. This equates to 16% of total expected VAT revenue of 26 member states (see European Commission, Press release MEMO/14/602, 23 October 2014, p. 3). For an example of the approach in calculating the tax gap, see S. Pisani, "Tax Gap and the Performance of the Italian Revenue Agency: An ongoing project", presentation at the International Tax Analysis Conference 2014, 20-21 January 2014, London.

In this respect, it is well known that the VAT intra-EU regime has raised significant concerns since its introduction on 1 January 1993. This system, which was supposed to last for four years only, has remained in force until now due to member states' failure to reach agreement on a definitive system based on taxation at the origin. The fundamental weak point of this system is the fact that taxation follows the principle of destination, so that goods circulate tax-free between member states. Whilst supplies are exempt of VAT in the member state of departure, these still qualify for a right to deduction or reimbursement of the VAT paid as input tax in that member state. As acknowledged by the European Court of Justice, because of the abolition of frontier within the Union, it is difficult for the tax authorities to satisfy themselves that the goods have or have not physically left the territory of the member state of departure. It is principally on the basis of the evidence provided by taxable persons (such as accounts, transport documents, invoices, settlement documents) and of their statements that the tax authorities so satisfy themselves.[72]

In order to compensate for the elimination of customs formalities and checks, and avoid losses of tax revenue, a computerised system for the automatic exchange of information on the value of intra-EU deliveries declared by traders was set up in each member state (VAT information exchange system or VIES). At the same time, a system (Intrastat) for collecting statistics on the movement of goods between the member states has been put in place. Moreover, a number of initiatives (for example, Fiscalis) and legislative measures have been introduced to facilitate cooperation among national administrations.[73] The magnitude of VAT losses shows, however, that such measures are not sufficient. As explained by the Commission, the VAT intra-EU regime gives member states "the illusion of having retained full sovereignty in determining their revenues and the

---

[72] See European Court of Justice, Case law C-409/04 Teleos and others v. Commissioners of Customs and Excise, [2007] ECR I-7797, paragraph 44. The European Commission has just unveiled five options for a future VAT system, based on the principle of destination, to replace the current temporary system (see European Commission, Press release IP/14/1216 of 30 October 2014).

[73] For example, there are provisions at EU level for mutual assistance between the member states, in particular concerning the recovery of taxes and the administrative cooperation in the field of VAT. Also, a guide on Risk Management for tax administrations has been established (see http://ec.europa.eu/taxation_customs/taxation/tax_cooperation/index_en.htm).

overall operation of the VAT system". In reality, however, they have no "certainty of being able to receive the revenues to which they are entitled".[74]

It should also be highlighted that the components of the VAT assessment base are equally at the origin of taxpayers' returns for direct taxation and social security contributions. The amounts at stake in these cases are, moreover, much higher than for VAT alone.[75] As the VAT base represents a kind of 'benchmark' for all tax returns, VAT avoidance generates a 'domino effect' on simultaneous avoidance of direct taxation revenue and social security contributions (Tremonti & Vitaletti, 1991:21). VAT avoidance is therefore no more than a component of a more general loss of tax revenue, putting at risk public finances and boosting the underground economy. In turn, the expansion of the latter has a negative impact on fair competition, upsetting in particular the conditions for a proper functioning of the internal market. Not least, VAT losses contribute to pushing up VAT rates (see later, Figure 7). The above discussion shows that the issue goes well beyond a simple question of budgetary losses.

VAT fraud spares no member state. This is due to the development and proliferation of sophisticated fraud mechanisms (like the 'carousel fraud'), which, taking advantage of the absence of internal borders, allows the launching of fraudulent operations 'touch-and-go'.[76] Yet, those same

---

[74] See European Commission, "A common system of VAT, A programme for the Single Market", COM (96) 328, Brussels, 22 July 1996, p. 25.

[75] See European Court of Auditors, "Special Report No 6/98 concerning the assessment of the system of resources based on VAT and GNP", point 4.3. A study undertaken by the Italian fiscal administration shows that €1 of VAT avoided triggers a further loss of €2.43 in direct taxation and social security contributions (see L. Abritta, D. Ballanti, R. Convenevole, C. Equizzi and S. Pisani, "Agenzia delle Entrate, Gli effetti dell'applicazione degli studi di settore nel biennio 1998-99", November 2003).

[76] In a 'carousel fraud' a so-called 'conduit company' (A) makes an exempt intra-community supply of goods to a 'missing trader' (B) in another member state. This company (B) acquires goods without paying VAT and subsequently makes a domestic supply to a third company (C), called the 'broker'. The 'missing trader' collects VAT on its sales to the 'broker', but does not pay the VAT to the Treasury and disappears. The 'broker' (C) claims a refund of the VAT on its purchases from B. Consequently, the financial loss to the Treasury equals the VAT paid by C to B. Subsequently, Company C may declare an exempt intra-EU supply to Company (A) and, in its turn, the latter may make an exempt intra-EU supply to (B) and the fraud

borders continue to exist for VAT national administrations whose cooperation in monitoring the compliance of intra–EU operations often proves to be difficult and not sufficiently timely. Not to mention the risk that national administrations could be reluctant to deploy efforts when a fraud has no budgetary effects in their own territory.

The European Parliament called on member states to commit to the target of reducing the tax gap by at least one-half by 2020. Parliament also called upon the Commission to launch a study on possible indicators constituting a basis for reducing tax fraud, evasion and avoidance and, if appropriate, to establish a standardised set of indicators for measuring tax evasion and avoidance.[77]

In this context, it might be worth considering a proposition whose initial intention was to show a possible way of moving from the current 'transitional' intra-EU VAT regime to a definitive VAT regime (taxation at origin as envisaged by the EU legislator).[78] This proposition draws from the Italian experience, where since 2005 VAT returns show both the tax assessment base and the VAT due, split between final consumers and taxable persons. VAT returns further allocate to each Italian region both the tax assessment base for final consumers and the tax due. Hence, VAT revenue can be attributed to each Italian region, on the basis of the actual final consumption as declared by taxable persons.

This set-up mirrors the two main features of this declaration framework. First, a geographical allocation of VAT paid out on the basis of the actual final consumption, as opposed to an allocation based on the place where the taxable person has his or her legal fiscal seat. Hence, VAT related to the purchase of a good can be allocated to the region where the sale has taken place, whereas previously it would have been allocated to the region of the legal seat of the seller. It is worth noting that this geographical allocation of VAT revenues is achieved without the need of statistical data. The latter come however into play in relation to the second feature of the

---

pattern resumes, thus explaining the term 'Carousel fraud' (see European Commission, "Report on the use of administrative cooperation arrangements in the fight against VAT fraud", COM (2004) 260 of 16 April 2004, p. 6).

[77] See European Parliament, Resolution of 12 December 2013 on the call for a measurable and binding commitment against tax evasion and avoidance in the EU.

[78] For the details of the proposition, see R. Convenevole, *Come approdare al regime definitivo dell'IVA nell'Unione Europea*, 2011 (www.ilmiolibro.it).

system, i.e. enlarging the scope for detection of VAT avoidance. It is a fact that the fight against fraud cannot imply rely on random investigations and has to be built into the return declaring system. In this respect, since fraud concentrates on final consumption, the possibility of comparing actual regionalised VAT consumption (on the basis of VAT returns) with 'household consumption' from statistical sources provides crucial information for assessing patterns of VAT fraud risks at 'regional' level.[79]

Such a model could also be of interest at EU level for the same reasons that reside at the basis of the Italian model, i.e. fiscal federalism and equity of burden-sharing among local administrative entities as well as the fight against VAT fraud. For example, concerning the latter, a comparison between administrative (VAT returns) and national accounts data clearly shows that in Italy the VAT gap is quite different from one region to another. Such comparisons provide a useful indication for risk-based controls. *Mutatis mutandis*, the same could happen at EU level, from one member state to another. For this to happen, VAT returns in all member states should provide a split of the taxable base and of the VAT due into two parts: domestic sales (divided by final consumers and taxable persons) and intra-EU (by country of destination).

The consideration of such model at EU level could provide better instruments to fight VAT fraud by providing tax administrations with more adequate information on intra-EU deliveries than is currently available. Several improvements could be obtained to the advantage of both the taxable persons and the fiscal administrations. For example, Intrastat declarations could be discontinued. The enhanced information available would improve the timely detection of fictitious operations, which are often a source of profit for organised crime, so as to reduce the possibility of engineering 'carousel frauds'. In turn, the opportunities to supply the underground economy with 'tax-free' goods will also be reduced. By focusing controls on an EU-wide risk basis, indiscriminate across-the-board controls could be reduced, and hence the burden on compliant taxable

---

[79] Similarly, as sketched in the proposed VAT-resource in the section entitled "Making the VAT-resource visible to citizens", the fact that taxable persons should identify in their periodic returns the part of final consumption subject to the national 'standard rate' might provide useful information for the fight against the fraud. A match with similar information from statistical sources would reveal the VAT 'gap' for standard-rated sales and therefore provide the initial input fiscal administrations require to conduct a backwards check through the whole VAT chain, from wholesale and production up to importation.

persons. All in all, increased compliance by taxable persons could be ensured, without imposing, at first sight, significant extra administrative costs.

Two categories of revenue sources for the EU budget

By stating that "The Union shall provide itself with the means necessary to attain its objectives and carry through its policies", and that "the budget shall be financed wholly from own resources", Article 311 TFEU does not prescribe the categories of resources to be tapped for funding the EU budget. It leaves this decision to the Council, which "may establish new categories of own resources or abolish an existing category".

In practice, two categories of resources could be envisaged. A first option would be, as is the case today for the GNI-based resource, to fund the EU budget through a levy from the cashbox of overall national taxation, without a link to any specific tax or individual taxpayers. A second possibility would be to allocate to the EU budget revenue raised from an explicit and visible fiscal source, for example as proposed by the European Commission with the FTT. Yet, these two options would entail quite different consequences.

The first option reflects the concept that funding the EU budget is an intergovernmental matter, whose details and financial consequences are an issue to be decided behind closed doors. As observed by the Commission, this would be functional to "an idea of the Union in which citizens would be represented purely indirectly by their Member States. The status of the EU as a Union of Member States and the citizens, which is currently reflected in the Treaty, would be abandoned on the financing side of the budget". In the end, "the special character of the EU, which is not a simple club of different members that are paying their membership fees", would be called into question.[80]

The second option would provide recognition that the European Union constitutes a new legal order of international law the subjects of which comprise not only member states but also their nationals. In this respect, the Treaty refers several times to the need to take decisions as openly and as closely as possible to the citizen and provides that the EU institutional

---

[80] See European Commission, COM (2004) 505 final of 14 July 2004, Vol. II, op. cit., p. 46, and SEC (2011) 876 of 27 October 2011, op. cit., p. 2.

framework should serve the interests of both the citizens and the member states.[81]

Transparency is another principle to be imbued in the implementation of the EU budget. There are multiple objectives associated with this principle: reinforcing institutional control and scrutiny over Union expenditure, enhancing the legitimacy of the administration and its accountability to the citizen and, last but not least, ensuring the visibility of Union action.[82] As a result, citizens should be able to know where, and for what purposes, EU funds are spent. For example, for the European Structural and Investment Funds, in order "to ensure transparency concerning support from the Funds", member states shall have a communication strategy for each operational programme and notably provide information to the public about the operations supported, including a summary for citizens of the content of implementation reports.[83]

A fiscal source to fund the EU budget would establish a parallelism between the right of citizens to be kept informed on the use of public funds and their equal right to be informed about the burden they support. As observed by the Commission, the lack of a direct relationship between citizens and the EU budget financing is a "manifestation of the 'democratic deficit'".[84] Moreover, as discussed in the section "What do 'own resources' actually mean?", member states' own budgetary documents provide an incomplete and not transparent accounting of their contributions to the EU budget. As a result, citizens' comprehension of the present system is

---

[81] See Articles 1 TEU, 10 TEU, 13(1) TEU, 15 TFEU and the Protocol (No. 2) on the application of the principles of subsidiarity and proportionality. It should be observed that with the Declaration of the European Council of Laeken (14-15 December 2001), the member states had already acknowledged that European citizens "feel that deals are all too often cut out of their sight and they want better democratic scrutiny" (Document SN 300/1/01 REV 1, p. 20). See also footnote 99.

[82] See Articles 34, 35 and 59(1) of Regulation (EU, EURATOM) No 966/2012, op. cit.

[83] See Articles 50(9), 115, 116, 117 and Annex XII of Regulation (EU) No 1303/2013 of the European Parliament and of the Council of 17 December 2013 (OJ L 347 of 20 December 2013). As an example, in Italy the web portal www.opencoesione.gov.it/ provides information on each project co-financed during the 2007-2013 programming cycle by Regions and State Central Administrations.

[84] See European Commission, COM (1998) 560 of 7 October 1998, op. cit., Annex II, p. 3.

virtually absent. They are therefore not stimulated to demand a proper account-giving on the funds spent, and thus pressure from public opinion plays a limited role in influencing the decision-makers. Visibility of EU revenue would go in the same direction as the requirement, set recently by the Treaties (Article 318 TFEU), aiming at a better demonstration of the added value of EU expenditure whose main rationale is to do more and better than the member states can do by themselves.[85]

Yet, as noted by Ehlermann (1982:586), a fiscal resource for the EU acquires a political dimension when it is made known to the taxpayer, and in particular where the member state collecting the tax acts in the name of the Union. Moreover, financing the EU budget through a direct entitlement of a fiscal source would be a critical decision with in practice no possible reversal. Shifting the liability of funding the EU budget from member states directly to citizens will open a breach in the consolidated 'intergovernmental' structure for setting EU revenue arrangements. As the 'equity' of contributions would have to be appreciated at the level of the individual citizens across Europe, rather than in a relationship between member states, such a shift will challenge the currently omnipresent concept of 'budgetary balances'. A first outcome would be a different burden-sharing at member state level as compared to today's situation. Also, since national administrations would be in charge of collecting EU revenue, their effectiveness in ensuring compliance by taxable persons will be a matter of growing attention at the EU level.[86]

Also, visibility of EU revenue will inevitably generate an increasing demand for an explanation of the choices underlying EU spending programmes and for evidence about the results and impacts actually achieved. In turn, this will prompt interrogations about who should be held accountable for the management of EU expenditure – a responsibility that is currently mostly shared between the Commission and a significant number of member states' bodies involved in the day-to-day management of EU

---

[85] See also the subsection entitled "The legitimacy of EU revenue". Concerning the accountability for implementing the EU budget, see Cipriani (2010).

[86] An EU right of scrutiny on the effectiveness of national VAT systems has already been recognised by the European Court of Justice. The latter has stated that since the current VAT resource is based on VAT revenue collected by member states, the EU level is entitled, for example, to examine the effectiveness of member states' mutual cooperation in fighting against fraud and tax avoidance (see European Court of Justice, Case law C-539/09 European Commission v. Federal Republic of Germany, Judgment of 15 November 2011).

funds. Some discomfort would inevitably be felt at the various management levels, not yet used to an accountability process encompassing an in-depth review of the results achieved.

Not least, the visibility of EU revenue might encourage the European Parliament, which today does not exercise much say in the revenue field, to question the current member states' absolute power. Yet, Parliament's accrued responsibilities on the revenue side could represent a positive development, as it should logically imply taking political responsibility vis-á-vis citizens for taxation decisions underlying its spending priorities. This would be a natural development of the extension of the co-decision framework for approving the spending programmes.

While, in principle, an EU fiscal resource would not be incompatible with 'budgetary discipline' (i.e. setting an own resources ceiling), its introduction could be seen as an initial step towards financial autonomy for the EU and the power to raise revenue at EU level. Asserting the right to decide autonomously on the volume of the resources for the EU budget could be the next step. History shows that Parliaments have won their spurs by obtaining the power to levy taxes.

Back to the past

The option of funding the EU budget through a levy from the cashbox of overall national taxation would keep the essence of the current system, but in a radically simplified way, thereby meeting the first of the review's four guiding principles (simplicity, transparency, equity and democratic accountability). Indeed, in a system where the overarching objective is to ensure an acceptable burden-sharing among member states on the basis of the 'budgetary balances' concept, there is a simpler solution than today's VAT and GNI-based resources. A burden-sharing key similar to that provided by Article 200 of the EEC founding Treaty could achieve the same result, at a far lower administrative cost and with the advantage that such key could be set and adjusted according to any suitable criteria. In particular, the burden-sharing key could easily take account of claims of imbalance by some member states. A single 'own resource' called "Financing the EU budget" could be created, with an entry in each member state's budget, hence ensuring more transparency compared to today's situation. This resource could also play the role of top-up resource to balance the budget.

One could imagine a key based on member states' share of EU GNI. However, as shown in the previous section "Who pays how much?", the current financing arrangements do not strictly reflect member states' share in the total EU GNI. This is due in particular to the UK rebate. Also, the use of GNI as accounting data as the basis of national contributions is not without difficulties, due to the challenge of meeting the required quality of data by member states' statistical processes (for example, the comparability of sources and methods and the exhaustiveness of GNI estimates). Yet, if GNI cannot be taken as an undisputed basis for EU revenue, the burden-sharing among member states could still be based on any other acceptable key, whether an approximation of the GNI share or other criteria. In this respect, column 3 of Table 5 and column 3 of Table 6 provide examples of what such keys might look like.

By reference to the other three guiding principles of the review (transparency, equity and democratic accountability), such option would in practice from the outset sacrifice transparency and democratic accountability. There would be at the very best a clearer presentation in national budgetary documents, although out of immediate reach of a large majority of citizens. Furthermore, 'equity' would be replaced by the concept of 'reasonable net contribution' for each member state, on the basis of highly questionable 'budgetary balances' calculations.

An EU revenue system taking the form of a burden-sharing key might certainly appear as a step backwards politically for the Union. However, borrowing the logic of the accounting principle of 'substance over legal form', a 'true and fair view' of the current EU revenue system would acknowledge that its underlying rationale is no more than finding an acceptable burden-sharing among member states. In fact, the option of 'resuscitating' a system of contribution scales similar to that provided for by Article 200 EEC could even represent a more 'European' solution than the current arrangements. Indeed, at that time the Council could modify the contribution scales by the unanimity rule, without further confirmation by national parliaments.

Making an EU resource visible to citizens

The requirement of transparency and democratic accountability set among the guiding principles of the review would be best met by establishing an explicit and visible link between citizens and a fiscal source.

The choice of a fiscal resource to directly fund the EU budget is potentially large. Since the 1970s, a significant number of propositions have been put forward either to replace or to supplement existing resources.[87] Many of the proposals, however, have the characteristics of earmarked taxes, linked to specific fiscal policy objectives. For this reason, such taxes would better fit in a national context, where the fiscal competence lies. In particular, funding a budget for 'Europeans' with taxes not displaying a clear link with EU policies would appear rather peculiar. Also, to a greater or lesser extent, the assessment basis of such taxes would be narrow and uncertain. They would necessarily involve new administrative costs, notably because new collection and control systems would have to be put in place.

As the experience with the FTT shows, creating a new tax is easier said than done. Moreover, a new tax just to fund the EU budget would probably be extremely unpopular. As discussed earlier, the EU does not have the power to raise taxes on its own. In this respect, several member states explicitly rejected the idea of creating an EU tax to finance the EU budget.[88] After all, was it not also the European Parliament that recognised in 2007 "that the time for a new European tax has not yet come in the short term"?[89]

Everything seems to indicate that the way towards a direct fiscal source for financing the EU budget should pass through an existing tax, as also suggested by the European Parliament.[90] In this respect, VAT seems an obvious choice as it is a general tax triggered by consumers' decisions, and it is charged on most goods and services. Due to its broad basis, VAT

---

[87] For example, Aviation sector tax; Resource based on emission auctioning in the context of the EU Emission Trading System (ETS); Tax on energy based on the revised Energy Taxation Directive; EU Corporate Income Tax (EUCIT); Excise duty on motor fuel for transport and other energy taxes; Excise duty on tobacco and alcohol; Tax on corporate profits; Tax on dealings in securities; Tax on transport or telecommunications services; Withholding tax on interest; ECB profits (seigniorage); Ecotax; Taxes on currency transactions; Tax on savings; Taxes on financial transactions.

[88] European Commission, "Reforming the Budget, Changing Europe: Short Summary of Contributions", SEC (2008) 2739, Brussels, 3 November 2008, point 3.1.

[89] See European Parliament, Resolution of 29 March 2007, op. cit., paragraph 37.

[90] The European Parliament proposed "the creation of a new system of own resources based on a tax already levied in the Member States, the idea being that this tax, partly or in full, would be fed directly into the EU budget as a genuine own resource, thus establishing a direct link between the Union and European taxpayers" (see European Parliament, Resolution of 29 March 2007, op. cit., paragraph 38).

provides a large and stable source of revenue. In 2012, VAT revenue accounted for some €927 billion, or 7.1% (weighted average) of the EU GDP.[91] VAT is thus a major source of revenue for national budgets, and in many member states, it is the most important. The majority of them have a standard rate at or above 20%. As shown below, the EU average VAT standard rate has risen strongly in recent years, from 19.5% in 2008 to 21.5% in 2014. This trend is explained by two main factors, namely the consequences of the financial and economic crisis and a longer-term shift towards indirect rather than direct taxation. In short, VAT as an EU own resource would be in line with member states' taxation patterns and trends.

Figure 7. Development of average standard VAT rate (EU-28, 2000-2014)

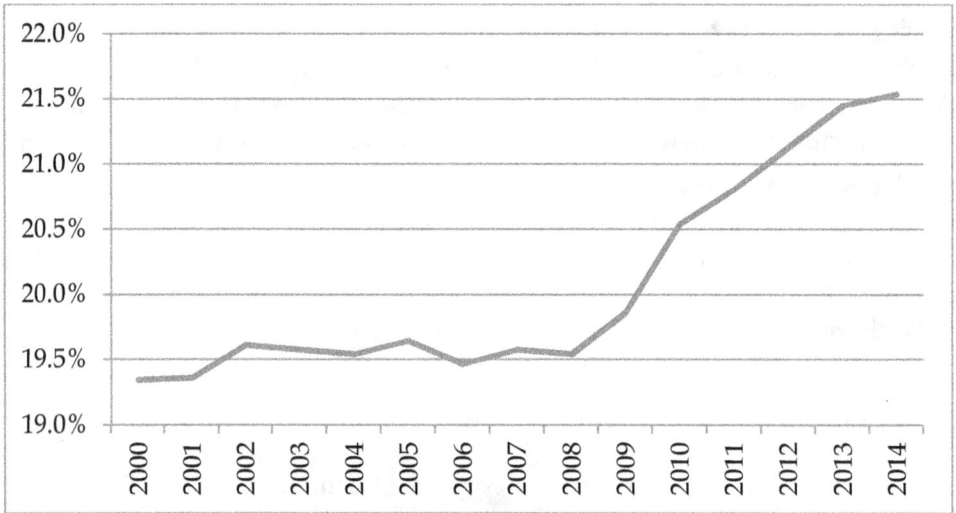

Source: European Commission, "Taxation trends in the European Union", Luxembourg, 2014, p. 25 (simple averages, value at 01.01 of each year).

The European Parliament has repeatedly expressed support for VAT as an own resource, giving several reasons for such a choice.[92] VAT was

---

[91] See European Commission, "Taxation trends in the European Union", Luxembourg, 2014, p. 179.

[92] In 1981, Parliament requested that "VAT should no longer be collected on the basis of statistical estimates, but on the basis of tax declarations…so that this source of revenue becomes a veritable Community VAT, parallel to the national VATs, because assessed on the same tax base, but levied at separate rates, independent of the national VAT rates" (see European Parliament, Resolution of 9 April 1981 on the

considered to represent the most reliable basis for own revenue, to be politically controllable, well known and familiar to the taxpayer and capable of being harmonised throughout the EU. A genuine VAT resource would represent a simple and transparent way to establish a link between the taxpayer and the destination of the tax. VAT revenue "is politically defensible as its yield is dependent on economic activity and economic growth".[93]

VAT would also fulfil to a large extent the guiding criteria for own resources identified by the Commission.[94] By setting a specific EU VAT rate, this tax might potentially represent for the EU a source of independent revenue and therefore of financial autonomy. The transparency of the tax would be ensured by the fact that it is borne ultimately (and visibly) by the final consumer, thus making possible a link with the citizen. Finally, VAT is ruled by European legislation since the late 1960s, when it was progressively introduced as a common tax area tailored to the Single Market. VAT therefore displays a clear relationship to EU policies.

Community's own resources, paragraph 13). The draft Treaty establishing the European Union (known as the Spinelli Treaty), adopted by Parliament in February 1984, confirmed the wish to finance the EU budget through a fixed percentage of the VAT basis (see Article 71, OJ C 77 of 19 March 1984, p. 50). This stance was reaffirmed in 1994, when Parliament proposed the creation, in place of the existing VAT and GNP resources, of a new source of revenue "which should take the form of a specified percentage of VAT ... directly imposed on the basis of tax declarations and denoted as such on invoices". Parliament pointed out that this would be "the most appropriate means of meeting the demands of being simple and transparent and constituting an effective link between the taxpayer and the destination of the tax (European Union)" (see European Parliament, Resolution of 21 April 1994 on a new system of own resources for the European Union, paragraphs 9 and 10; see also European Parliament Resolutions of 29 March 2007, op. cit., paragraphs 22 and 39; of 13 June 2012, op. cit., paragraph 3; and of 23 October 2012, op. cit., paragraph 74(4)).

[93] See the European Parliament report (Rapporteur H. Langes) on the "System of Own resources in the European Union", document A3-0228/94, 8 April 1994, paragraph 24, p. 15.

[94] The Commission has identified the following criteria: Sufficiency, Stability, Financial autonomy, Transparency, Link to EU policy, Fiscal equivalence, Internalising externalities, Subsidiarity principle, Limiting operating costs, Fairness at the level of member states, Horizontal and vertical equity for the taxpayers (see European Commission, SEC (2011) 876 of 27 October 2011, op. cit., p. 13).

As discussed earlier, the proposal of a VAT-based resource presented by the Commission in 2004 would have provided a solution to a major drawback of the current system, i.e. the absence of a direct and visible link to EU citizens. Drawing on this proposal, and in line with the subsidiarity and proportionality principles, one could actually envisage a VAT-based resource operating in 'symbiosis' with the national VAT system. Key features like the regulatory framework underlying the assessment basis, the management of the tax and its collection could rest with the national bodies. As a result, no dual system will need to be created.

The VAT-based resource would not represent a true tax but a kind of 'simil tax', with the following main characteristics:

- The VAT-based resource would take the form of an EU VAT rate, offset by a corresponding decrease of the national VAT rate. Therefore, the VAT-based resource would be financially neutral for the final consumer. As a result, no modification of the structure of prices or of the behaviour of economic agents should be expected.
- The EU VAT rate could be set in the own resources decision as an overall 'ceiling', thus respecting member states' constitutional requirements. The actual rate (possibly lower) would be established in the frame of the annual budgetary procedure.
- The EU VAT rate would apply on the value of final consumption of goods and services only. In this way, the VAT-based resource could weigh on the true economic impact of VAT and free itself of specific requirements of the VAT chain (in particular the right for deduction).
- Being a levy on final consumption, the EU VAT rate should apply in principle to all goods and services.[95] However, since in several member states a number of basic goods and services are subject to reduced and zero VAT rates, it would seem more 'politically' acceptable to apply the EU VAT rate only on goods and services that

---

[95] An earlier Commission's proposal of a VAT-based resource followed the same logic. Member states' VAT taxable base on which the 1% levy would have been applied included zero-rated goods and services (see European Commission, "Report on the Financing of the Community Budget", COM (87) 101, Brussels, 28 February 1987, p. 25 and 28). As a matter of fact, the assessment basis of the current VAT-based resource is meant to include ultimately the value of all transactions liable to VAT, irrespective of the rates applied (see footnote 14).

are subject to the national 'standard rate' (estimated to represent two-thirds of the VAT base).

- To allow the calculation of the amount due to the EU, taxable persons should identify in their periodical returns the part of final consumption subject to the national 'standard rate'.[96] Similarly, they should identify the EU VAT rate as part of the national rate in their invoices and fiscal receipts (see further the example in Figure 8). VAT payments arrangements to the national Treasury by taxable persons would not be affected.

- Member states would pay to the EU an amount equivalent to the EU VAT rate applied on the final consumption at the national 'standard rate', as shown in taxable persons' VAT returns. This should represent an incentive for national tax administrations to collect VAT revenue in full. Also, the VAT resource would fluctuate (upwards or downwards) with national consumption, thus putting the EU budget in line with economic circumstances.

The following table shows how the EU VAT rate (1% in the example) would apply to two member states, each of them having three different VAT rates. It can be seen that the EU share will accrue from standard-rated goods and services only. The difference of VAT rates between member states will have no influence in the amount to be transferred to the EU.

Table 9. An EU VAT rate

	VAT rate	Taxable base (€)	VAT resource (€)	VAT rate	Taxable base (€)	VAT resource (€)	Standard VAT rate	Taxable base (€)	VAT resource (€)	Total VAT resource (€)
Member state A	0%	100	0	5%	1,000	0	20%	10,000	100	100
Member state B	3%	150	0	6%	1,500	0	15%	10,000	100	100

Source: Author's own calculations.

With reference to the review's four guiding principles (simplicity, transparency, equity and democratic accountability), it is assumed that the requirement of transparency and democratic accountability will be met by creating an explicit and visible link between citizens and a fiscal source to

[96] The alternative, consisting of in establishing the assessment basis for the EU share through statistical data, would create the kind of difficulties experienced for the current VAT and GNI-based resources, including a significant administrative cost.

fund the EU budget. A further key element of transparency is the fact that the VAT-based resource will result directly from taxable persons' returns and not from a statistical calculation.

In a context in which the EU budget is designed for the benefit of all Europeans and is therefore funded by the latter through a direct and visible contribution, the equity of the system should be assessed at the level of EU citizens. It might be observed in this respect that member states' VAT assessment bases are not fully harmonised, notably due to VAT exemptions, differences in the scope of taxation and modalities to exert the right of deduction. Moreover, there are important divergences in the share of final consumption subject to the standard rate, ranging from about 40% to more than 90% according to the member state. This is notably due to national fiscal policies reflected in the application of reduced and zero-rates in some countries. An EU VAT rate as part of the standard rate could therefore create for final consumers with strictly similar consumption patterns an unequal treatment on the basis of their residence.

It should be stressed that introducing a direct and visible source for financing the EU budget would represent first and foremost the outcome of a political decision aimed at enhancing the role of European citizens in the EU decision process, by acknowledging their role as subjects of the Union as reflected in the Treaties. The achievement of such objective should take account of different principles (in particular, citizenship, transparency, equality, subsidiarity and proportionality), and therefore of a number of requirements whose concurrent fulfilment should be guided by the need to place the law at the service of what is realistically possible.

Reaching a full harmonisation of the VAT taxable basis is a complex process that would need time to materialise. Moreover, according to Article 113 TFEU, the harmonisation of indirect taxation should be pursued "to the extent that such harmonisation is necessary to ensure the establishment and the functioning of the internal market and to avoid distortion of competition". Full harmonisation is therefore not an end in itself and the differences existing among the member states should be deemed justified by objective grounds, in line with the applicable legislation.

Setting-up an ad-hoc harmonised base just for the purpose of a VAT resource would not be without a number of difficulties. For example, the harmonisation of the base of the current VAT-resource is achieved through complex calculations and is a source of the current system's opacity. The option, put forward by the Commission in 2011 in the framework of its proposal for a VAT-based resource, of establishing an EU-wide 'common' basket of standard-rated goods and services would also be rather complicated to put in place. Most importantly, both of the above options would not provide a direct link with the taxpayer.

It may also be noted that harmonisation of the assessment basis and 'equity' are not necessarily correlated. In today's revenue set-up, despite a full harmonisation in principle of the VAT assessment base, the VAT rate is 'uniform' in name only, as a lower rate or a capping of the base is applied to some member states. The consequence is precisely a difference among EU citizens in terms of per capita contributions depending on their place of residence.

In the current circumstances, and in line with the nature of 'simil tax' of the VAT-based resource designed as a tax-sharing mechanism, the equity for EU citizens should be ensured by applying the EU VAT rate to the same goods and services within the scope of the national standard rate. Such parallelism would free EU VAT revenue from an arbitrary exercise of judgment as the impact of the differences in the scope of application of standard-rated transactions among member states would simply reflect national fiscal policies, meant to be established in compliance with the VAT framework. One may refer, in a different context, to the EU direct aid to farmers whose level, despite the objective of excluding "any discrimination between producers or consumers within the Union" (Article 40(2) TFEU), may vary considerably from one farm to another, from one country to another or from one region to another. This shows that the achievable degree of harmonisation may be limited by objective factors, reflected in member states' policies in view of taking account of specific situations.

In fact, treating different situations identically is just as discriminatory as treating similar situations differently. Applying the EU VAT rate also to zero-rated transactions would create de facto a 'tax' on those transactions, whilst the objective of the EU VAT rate, as sketched above, is to be neutral for final consumers. A parallelism between the EU and national VAT standard rate would also avoid a kind of 'fiscal schizophrenia' in financing the EU and national budgets, while they are both funded by the same taxpayers. As provided for by the Treaties (Article 9 TEU and Article 20 TFEU), "Citizenship of the Union shall be additional to and not replace national citizenship". There is only one taxpayer.

Furthermore, even in the most optimistic scenario of an EU VAT rate of 2%, the bulk of VAT revenue will continue to derive from the application of national VAT rates, hence on the basis of the place of consumption. Assuming that the VAT standard rate applies to two-thirds of member states' VAT base, the EU share at an EU VAT rate of 2% would represent some €80 billion/year (or, per capita, an average contribution to the EU budget close to €160), while the overall VAT revenue is in the order of €927 billion/year (2012). This means that in relative terms the impact of the EU VAT rate would not be such as to upset significantly EU citizens' fiscal burden.

Finally, linking EU revenue from VAT to the economic trend will create a parallelism with national budgets. As envisaged 20 years ago by the Langes report, and most interestingly in the current economic context: "If national economies stagnate (as at present) both the Member States and the Union would have to economise."[97] This means that the requirement of a balanced budget might not have to be achieved in all circumstances through a top-up resource; a reduction of expenditure could also be considered. This is an issue that should be part of the annual budgetary procedure debate, in the light of the outcome of an on-going monitoring of expected results and lessons learned of the various spending programmes. While it is understandable that predictability is necessary in multiannual programmes, this principle cannot justify a member state's 'drawing right' despite poor results, only because the overall MFF agreement is meant to be a global financial package. The EU added-value concept, i.e. that the *raison d'être* of EU funds is to achieve objectives beyond the member states' reach, should be without exception. In this respect, visibility of EU revenue will help in refuting the false idea that EU funds 'grow on trees' and that they therefore constitute a kind of 'manna' to be taken advantage of.

Concerning 'simplicity', the VAT resource sketched above would require taxable persons to identify in their periodical returns the part of final consumption subject to the national 'standard rate'. Similarly, they will have to identify the EU VAT rate as part of the national rate in their invoices and fiscal receipts. Since such information should be readily available to taxable persons, it is unlikely that this new requirement would have an appreciable impact on their compliance costs.[98] As shown below in the example of Figure 8, retailers are accustomed to deliver a receipt for each purchase showing not just the final price paid by customers but also the taxable amount per rate, the VAT rate and the VAT amount payable. It would be sufficient to slightly

---

[97] See footnote 93. According to Mr Langes, in the event of unforeseeable circumstances, a deficit should also be permitted, although temporary and under strict conditions.

[98] As matter of fact, VAT returns in Italy already provide such information.

'enhance' this information in the receipts by indicating that part of the VAT incorporated in the final price (1% in the example) will accrue to the EU.

A final (but critical) issue concerns avoiding giving the impression to citizens that with the introduction of a EU VAT rate they would pay an higher tax than it is currently the case, while the aim is precisely to substitute the current national contributions. Indeed, the combination of 'European' and 'tax' could be seen as an additional burden and could therefore become deeply unpopular. This is a further reason for not applying the EU VAT rate to zero-rated transactions, as in that case the impact would be to increase taxation for the citizen. As shown by the following figure, this problem could be avoided by making clear (as shown in the white text against a dark background) that the overall VAT taxation will remain the same.

One might actually argue that the principles of transparency and taxation by consent make visibility of EU revenue an objective in itself. Even in the current national contributions-based system, some progress towards transparency would be possible. Failing the possibility to refer to a specific taxable basis resulting from an EU VAT rate, fiscal receipts could already be used as a 'vehicle' to convey a message such as: "an amount equal to [0.30]% of the VAT assessment base is transferred to the EU budget".

Such forms of visibility would not need to wait until an explicit legal requirement is introduced. The 30-year link, although hidden, between VAT revenue collected by member states and funding the EU budget, would certainly legitimise the Commission to 'encourage' the introduction of forms of visibility for citizens, along the lines of the example in Figure 8. This could take the form of a specific recommendation following Article 292 TFEU, like the Commission did to encourage and facilitate the dissemination of information for voters on the occasion of the recent elections to the European Parliament.[99]

---

[99] See the Commission recommendation of 12 March 2013 on enhancing the democratic and efficient conduct of the elections to the European Parliament (OJ L 79 of 21 March 2013, p. 29). The Commission has stressed the need to ensure that democratic control and accountability occur at the level at which decisions are taken. In that perspective, the recommendation recalls that decisions shall be taken as openly and as closely as possible to the citizens, in view of reinforcing the democratic legitimacy of the EU decision-making process. Bringing the system closer to Union citizens, so the recommendation is a necessary corollary to closer institutional integration and an efficient means to bridge the divide between politics and citizens of the Union (see 'Whereas' 1, 2, 4, 9, 10).

One may actually expect that such measures could be imposed by themselves as a 'best practice', favoured by pressure from citizens and consumer organisations. Moreover, these measures could be implemented progressively, without an absolute need to introduce them in all member states and at the same time.

Figure 8. Making visible the VAT accruing to the EU budget

```
            ------------------------------------
            CHK#  46         TBL#  6
                              #  9905
            02/02/2014 19:31:53      GUESTS   2
            ------------------------------------
                   2 P.Margherita        14.90
                   1 Peroni Small         3.75
                   1 Coke                 2.30
            SUBTOTAL:                    20.95
            Terminal B          ---------------
            TOTAL:                     £20.95

            Sales-VAT  VAT Rate  VAT Amt    Total
               17.46    20.00%     3.49    20.95
            EU Budget    [1.00%]     [0.17]
            Food excl Set Menus           14.90
            Drink excl Set Menus           6.05
            ------------------------------------
            Last Serviced      02/02/2014 20:07:26
            ------------------------------------

               Tips & Gratuities are discretionary
              except for groups of 8 or more where an
              optional service charge of 10% has been
                             added.




                    And everyday you could
                    win a free meal for 2
```

Concluding remarks

The current EU revenue system allows a stable flow of resources, in line with the MFF agreement. The best guarantee in this respect is that some 90% of these resources are handed back to member states in the form of EU expenditure. Yet, there are good reasons for reform, as this system does not score well against key criteria: simplicity, transparency, equity and democratic accountability. In particular, whilst the EU budget is financed through overall national taxation, the EU financial resources do not ensure a visible link with the taxpayers, leaving them in the dark. As a result, EU revenue arrangements are not consistent with the principles of transparency and taxation by consent.

The Commission's attempt to reform the EU revenue system for the MFF 2014-2020 was not successful, so that the status quo was the only course left. It should, however, be observed that the Commission's proposals did not seek to provide a solution to the opacity of the system. Disavowing a prior proposition that would have established an explicit link with the taxpayer, the new VAT resource would have continued to be perceived as a national expenditure. Visibility was equally not a main concern of the Commission proposal for introducing a FTT. Moreover, this proposal raised consistent opposition from a number of member states fearing that, on balance, the overall impact of such tax would have been negative. Also, complex issues have arisen and the potential for revenue proved to be uncertain. Finally, the proposition for granting a correction mechanism to some member states lacked transparency about its underlying justification, hence hindering an assessment of its fairness.

There seem to exist two main options for reforming the EU revenue system, i.e. a 'member-states centred' system and a system based on citizens' direct liability. The first option could consist of coming back to the arrangements of the early days of the EEC Treaty, i.e. to set a burden-sharing key by member state. The EU revenue system could be easily fine-tuned, for example by reference to the current burden-sharing. The system would become definitively simpler (no need for the current VAT and GNI-based resources) and more predictable in its impact. It could notably incorporate any kind of correction that should be deemed necessary for any member state. Administrative work would be reduced to a minimum. Yet, such option would in practice sacrifice from the outset the requirements for transparency and democratic accountability. Furthermore, the 'equity' criteria would be replaced by the concept of 'reasonable net contribution' for each member state, on the basis of the highly questionable 'budgetary balances' calculations. Still, this alternative would be a way of killing two birds with one stone: a radical simplification of the revenue system while preserving fundamentally the status quo as member states will remain the (pay)masters. Such an option might certainly appear as a political step backwards. However, the underlying rationale of the current system is no more than finding an acceptable burden-sharing key among member states.

Finding a fiscal source to make individuals directly liable would be the second option. In this respect, VAT represents an obvious choice also because it would avoid creating an ad-hoc tax to fund the EU budget. A VAT-based resource could be set as a 'simil tax', operating in 'symbiosis' with the national VAT system and without the need to create a parallel system. Key features, such as the regulatory framework underlying the assessment basis, the management of the tax and its collection, could remain the responsibility of national bodies. Moreover, the EU revenue generated could follow the income trend, so as to create a parallelism with economic circumstances (notably in the case of economic stagnation).

This resource would be based on an EU VAT rate as part of the national rate, thus ensuring visibility whilst keeping the fiscal burden unchanged for the final consumer. Such an option would undoubtedly meet the requirement of transparency and democratic accountability. To prepare the ground towards these objectives, the Commission could also envisage as an initial step encouraging member states and economic operators to introduce forms of transparency in fiscal receipts through a specific recommendation. Such a measure could actually be imposed by itself as a 'best practice'.

The equity of the VAT resource should be considered at the level of the citizens, as the ones directly supporting the burden rather than through an accounting balance between member states. Equity for EU citizens should be ensured by the fact that the EU rate would be applied to standard rated goods and services, within the scope of each national system. Such parallelism would also avoid a kind of 'fiscal schizophrenia' in financing the EU and national budgets while they are both funded by the same taxpayers.

Concerning 'simplicity', taxable persons would be required to provide some further information that should be readily available, hence not implying appreciable compliance costs on business.

Yet, financing the EU budget through a direct entitlement on VAT revenue, although minimal, would be a critical decision with in practice no possible reversal. It might potentially generate a number of far-reaching consequences. The effectiveness of national administrations in collecting EU revenue and ensuring compliance by taxable persons will be a matter of growing interest for the EU level. The more so as the magnitude of the VAT gap is such that its negative impact goes beyond budgetary consolidation and also affects the functioning of the internal market.

Shifting the liability of funding the EU budget from member states directly to citizens might encourage moves, notably by the European Parliament, to seek greater influence in the revenue field and assert a right of autonomous decision at EU level on the volume of the resources for the EU budget. Yet, Parliament's accrued responsibilities on the revenue side could represent a positive development as it should logically imply taking political responsibility towards citizens for taxation decisions underlying its spending priorities.

Visibility of EU revenue would most likely provoke a volley of questions from citizens, such as: What is the purpose of the EU budget? Whom profits from it? On whom does the burden fall? Who is managing EU expenditure and who is ultimately accountable for the results? Visibility of EU revenue could well be the detonator of an unprecedented debate about the EU budget, and ultimately about Europe as such. In short, visibility of EU revenue would doubtless represent a significant political choice.

The two options sketched above bear witness to different visions. Yet, a drastic choice between the two options may not be the best way to progress towards a new EU revenue system. Since the EU is a Union of member states and their citizens, realism would recommend paying attention to concerns from both sides. In this perspective, a new EU revenue system could be built on a combination of 'visible' and 'invisible' resources, by financing in an initial stage the EU budget in equal parts through a VAT-based resource, made visible to citizens, and a simple national contribution that could be used also as a top-up resource. This latter resource could be based either on the EU GNI share, or on any other acceptable burden-sharing key.

3. EU EXPENDITURE: THE OTHER SIDE OF THE SAME COIN

As pointed out by the European Commission, "The funding must deliver the expected results – public authorities do not have an 'entitlement' to receive funds to spend as they wish, rather they receive EU funding to help them deliver on commonly agreed EU objectives". In this respect, the Council recently recalled that "better spending and sound financial management of EU funds is of a particular importance for the public perception of actions financed from the EU budget".[100]

A key argument used against the introduction of a fiscal source for the EU budget is that it would create hostility on the part of the public and it would end up decreasing its support for the EU. Indeed, the context seems far from being favourable as polls reveal that the majority of Europeans say that the EU budget "gives poor value for money for EU citizens" (44%, versus 27% saying that it provides "good value for money").[101] It should also be added that a side-effect of the current 'opaque' system is to create confusion about the actual volume of the EU budget, which is often overemphasised.

The fear of provoking negative reactions on the part of the public, although understandable, is tantamount to admitting that the policies financed from the EU budget do not produce sufficiently convincing results

---

[100] See European Commission, "A Budget for Europe 2020", COM (2011) 500, Brussels, 29 June 2011, part I, pp. 8-9, and Council recommendation on the discharge to be given to the Commission for the financial year 2012, doc. 5848/14 ADD 1, Brussels, 5 February 2014, Introduction, point 4.

[101] See Standard Eurobarometer 75, "Europeans and the European Union budget", May 2011, p. 8
(http://ec.europa.eu/public_opinion/archives/eb/eb75/eb75_budg_en.pdf).

about their added value. Nevertheless, this cannot be the ground for keeping the EU budget financing out of citizens' sight. The need to convincingly demonstrate whether and to what extent the achievements of EU expenditure have met the expectations exist, irrespective of the visibility of revenue arrangements. Moreover, in the context of the current weak accountability performance, a visible fiscal source for the EU budget would serve the function of increasing the pressure on the management to demonstrate the added value of EU expenditure, thus potentially enhancing the public's trust in the EU's finances.

Public support can only be acquired by funding effective policies that work to the advantage of the European citizens as a whole. Producing tangible results that entail an added value for Europeans could only facilitate their acceptance of the corresponding taxation.[102] Failing this, the legitimacy of the EU budget itself will inevitably be cast into doubt, regardless whether it is or not funded by a visible fiscal source.

Undeniably, as pointed out by the European Parliament, a reform of revenue cannot lose sight of the expenditure side of the budget.[103] It would seem in particular that the following interlinked issues also deserve consideration in the framework of the current review of the EU revenue system: the legitimacy of EU revenue and the volume of resources potentially needed for the EU budget.

The legitimacy of EU revenue

The Treaties establish a causality link between, on one side, the Union's competences and the objectives to be attained and, on the other side, the financial means necessary to attain these objectives.[104] The Treaties further

---

[102] For the Commission's analysis of the 'EU added value' concept see European Commission, "The added value of the EU budget", SEC (2011) 867, Brussels, 29 June 2011. For a discussion on this issue, see Tarschys (2005) and Cipriani (2007 and 2010).

[103] See European Parliament, Resolution of 29 March 2007 , op. cit., paragraphs 14 and 34. Also, in its Resolution of 25 March 2009 on the Mid-Term Review of the 2007-2013 Financial Framework, Parliament pointed out that the reform of revenue and a review of expenditure "should be run in parallel with the aim of merging them in a global and integrated reform for a new system of EU financing and spending at the latest for the MFF starting in 2016/2017"(see paragraph 9).

[104] See Articles 3(6) TEU and 311 TFEU.

specify that in areas that do not fall within its exclusive competence, the Union's action is restricted to objectives that member states cannot sufficiently achieve by themselves and therefore management at the EU level would be the most cost-effective way (criteria of need-for-action or subsidiarity principle).[105] Finally, in support of the previous condition, "[t]he reasons for concluding that a Union objective can be better achieved at Union level shall be substantiated by qualitative and, wherever possible, quantitative indicators".[106]

In particular, a relevant assessment of performance for a spending programme should refer to the usual relationship $input \Rightarrow output \Rightarrow outcome \Rightarrow impact$. The means needed for the implementation of a programme should be put in relation to its deliverables, immediate effects and long-term changes in society that are attributable to the EU's action.[107] This would require designing spending programmes in terms of specific, measurable and achievable objectives, expected outcomes and resulting costs.

A 'critical mass' of necessary funds constitutes a crucial factor to achieve a precise and identifiable result. It may be observed in this respect that the EU budget intervenes in some 40 spending areas. Table 10 below lists the nine EU spending programmes that have been allocated by the MFF 2014-2020 appropriations for more than €1 billion/year on average.

---

[105] See Article 5(3) TEU.

[106] See Article 5 of the Protocol (no 2) on the application of the principles of subsidiarity and proportionality. The Financial Regulation No. 966/2012, op. cit., establishes a link between 'value for money' and the setting of performance indicators in such a way that results can be assessed for each activity (see Articles 30(3) and 38(3)(e)). This information should be provided annually to the European Parliament and the Council.

[107] The following definitions are given by the "Glossary of Key Terms in Evaluation and Results Based Management" (see OECD, Development Assistance Committee, Paris, 2002). 'Inputs': the financial, human, and material resources used for the development intervention. 'Outputs': the products, capital goods and services that result from a development intervention; changes resulting from the intervention that are relevant to the achievement of outcomes may also be included. 'Outcomes': the likely or achieved short-term and medium-term effects of an intervention's outputs. 'Impacts': positive and negative, primary and secondary long-term effects produced by a development intervention, directly or indirectly, intended or unintended.

Table 10. MFF 2014-2020 – Main spending programmes (€ million, Commitment appropriations, 2011 prices)

MFF Heading	Programme	Appropriations	Average/year	% of MFF
(1)	(2)	(3)	(4)	(5)
Economic, social and territorial cohesion	Cohesion Policy	325,146	46,449	36.19
Sustainable Growth: Natural Resources	European Agricultural Guarantee Fund (EAGF) — Market related expenditure and direct payments	277,851	39,693	30.93
Sustainable Growth: Natural Resources	European Agricultural Fund for Rural Development (EAFRD)	84,936	12,134	9.45
Competitiveness for growth and jobs	Horizon 2020	70,200	10,029	7.81
Competitiveness for growth and jobs	Connecting Europe Facility	19,300	2,757	2.15
Global Europe	Development Cooperation Instrument (DCI)	17,390	2,484	1.94
Global Europe	European Neighbourhood Instrument (ENI)	13,683	1,955	1.52
Competitiveness for growth and jobs	Education, Training, Youth and Sport (Erasmus +)	13,010	1,859	1.45
Global Europe	Instrument for Pre-accession assistance (IPA)	10,380	1,483	1.16
Total		831,896	118,842	92.60

Source: Author's own elaboration from European Commission, DG Budget (http://ec.europa.eu/budget/mff/figures/index_en.cfm#documents). Column 5 refers to total commitment appropriations less 'administration', 'compensations', 'other' and 'margins'.

The bulk of these appropriations is concentrated on Agriculture and Cohesion spending.[108] The remaining around 30 programmes will share among them slightly more than 7% of the MFF resources. For 20 of those programmes, yearly funds available vary from €18 million to €185 million. This means that if it is often quite difficult to demonstrate the actual impact and benefits brought by major spending programmes like 'Cohesion policy', it will be even more challenging for far smaller programmes to demonstrate the actual outcomes and impacts of EU expenditure.[109]

EU spending programmes pursue a multiplicity of grand objectives, often unrelated to the available funding and with no specific expected achievements. Parliament has expressed concern over the fact that the present budgetary cycle "tends to add one priority after another without taking any political decision as to issues that, given the limited resources available from the tax-payer, need to be scaled down in order to give way to the most crucial priorities".[110]

There is a risk of separated vertical strategies with limited or no synergies among the various strands and, not least, with the difficulty of drawing crosscutting conclusions. Objectives from high-level policy or legislative documents are often not sufficiently focused to allow for the monitoring of their achievement over time (for example, with milestones). There is no reliable system for collecting performance data in order to identify and report on results and impacts, as they become available.

---

[108] 'Cohesion policy' aggregates different objectives of the 2014-2020 MFF, such as Regional convergence (Less developed regions), Competitiveness (More developed regions), Transition regions, Territorial cooperation, Youth Employment Initiative (specific top-up allocation), Outermost and sparsely populated regions as well as the Cohesion fund.

[109] Despite being an EU policy for 40 years and one of the most significant in terms of funding, according to polls very few people are informed about EU regional support: only slightly over one-third of EU respondents (34%) have heard about EU co-financed projects and almost two-thirds (64%) have not heard about any such project. See Flash Eurobarometer 384, Citizens' awareness and perceptions of EU Regional Policy, September 2013 (http://ec.europa.eu/public_opinion/flash/fl_384_sum_en.pdf).

[110] See European Parliament, Resolution of 25 March 2009 on the ABB-ABM method as a management tool for allocating budgetary resources, paragraph 13.

EU spending programmes are either entitlement programmes, in which the beneficiaries only have to meet certain conditions (like direct payments to farmers), or 'input'-based, in which EU disbursements are only linked to the 'eligibility' of the expenditure incurred. As discussed earlier, the MFF is a single 'package' where the relationship between national contributions and expenditure is based on the 'net-balances' approach, first as a measure to negotiate the agreement, and afterwards to monitor its implementation. Yet, this approach favours "instruments with geographically pre-allocated financial envelopes, rather than those with the greatest EU added value".[111] As a result, some 70% of the 2014-2020 MFF expenditure is directly or de facto pre-allocated on a country basis as part of the MFF.[112] In turn, 'geographical' allocation makes 'spending' an implicit objective and possibly the main one (Cohesion policy and Rural development are typical examples). To the point that the rate of funds 'absorption' plays the rather peculiar role of indicator of a programme's success. As if 'spending' was enough to achieving cost-effective and sustainable results.

In this respect, it is sometimes argued that when EU funds are associated with national co-financing (for example, in Cohesion policy and Rural development), there is a guarantee for effective spending as opposed to simple absorption of funds, since member states would take care to avoid wasting their own funds. Yet, the implication of a pre-allocation of EU funds on a geographical basis is that they 'must' be spent within a given timescale; otherwise, they will be lost (dictated by the decommitment rule) and most likely cause political embarrassment, notably at national level. There is therefore an objective incentive to 'fill' the national quota with whatever projects comply with the eligibility rules.

The recent introduction of ex-ante conditionalities (such as strategies and priority plans, administrative capacity, monitoring mechanisms) for Cohesion policy funds is deemed to ensure that at member state level the right conditions for spending are in place from the outset, so as to allow an effective and efficient achievement of the objectives of the programmes and thus results. Yet, the assurance on the adequacy of national systems through

---

[111] See European Commission, Press release MEMO/11/468, 29 June 2011, p. 7.

[112] Reference is made to Agricultural market-related expenditure and direct payments, Rural Development, Fisheries and Cohesion.

the Commission's ex-ante conditionalities assessment, which is currently on-going, will depend very much on the depth of this examination.

The Commission has indicated that its ambition for the 2014-2020 programming period "is to spend differently, with more emphasis on results and performance".[113] A similar statement was made for the previous MFF, with the intention "to maximise the impact of our common policies so that we further enhance the added value of every euro spent at European level" with a view also to "better assess Community value added".[114] The concept of EU added value is precisely the 'watershed' between national and EU budgets. Their roles are complementary but different. Not every expenditure entails an EU added value and the EU budget cannot intervene in all areas. In other words, prioritisation is a must. This is why defined needs, clear objectives and appropriate monitoring are the necessary corollaries of the subsidiarity principle.

Reporting by the European Commission on EU expenditure achievements is foreseen by four main requirements. A first occasion is represented by the preparation of the budget for the following year. In this context, programmes statements should contain information on the achievement of all specific, measurable, achievable, relevant and timed objectives previously set for the various activities, as well as new objectives measured by indicators.[115] After budget implementation, there are three further requirements. These refer to i) the report on budgetary and financial management, which includes the achievement of the objectives for the year, in accordance with the principle of sound financial management;[116] ii) the annual activity reports of its Directors-General (together with the summary

---

[113] See European Commission, COM (2011) 500 of 29 June 2011, op. cit., part I, p. 9.

[114] See European Commission, "Building our common future: Policy challenges and budgetary means of the enlarged Union 2007–13", COM (2004) 101, Brussels, 26 February 2004, p. 3 and p. 30.

[115] See Articles 30(3) and 38(3)(e) of the Financial Regulation (EU, Euratom) No 966/2012, op. cit.

[116] See Article 142 of the Financial Regulation (EU, Euratom) No 966/2012, op. cit., and Article 227 of Commission Delegated Regulation (EU) No 1268/2012 of 29 October 2012 (OJ L 362, 31 December 2012, p. 1).

adopted by the Commission);[117] and iii) the evaluation report on the Union's finances introduced by the Lisbon Treaty.[118]

Due to the weak performance context discussed above, these reporting instruments failed so far to provide sufficient, relevant and reliable evidence on what the EU's expenditure has achieved. In particular:

- The programmes statements of operation expenditure provide extensive information on the context where EU funds are allocated and, when they exist (such as for Europe 2020), of the overall policy targets. Although it is admitted that it is rarely possible to determine whether the desired result is a direct consequence of the policy intervention, as other factors not under the control of the European Commission also influence outcomes.

- The report on budgetary and financial management is limited in practice to the rates of expenditure achieved and contains no performance information.

- While the Commission's Directors-General annual activity reports "shall indicate the results of the operations by reference to the objectives set" as well as "the use made of the resources provided",[119] the information on policy achievements is quite limited, notably in case of policies (about 80% of the EU budget) whose day-to-day management is ensured by member states' bodies. The information provided in the annual activity reports is either derived from member states' data, whose accuracy and reliability might be variable, or it is based on simulations of the cumulative expected impact on GDP and employment elaborated by macroeconomic models that cannot be considered as evidence for actual results. Evaluations also represent a source of information, but they remain experts' studies not endorsed by the Commission. In fact, EU funds

---

[117] See Article 66(9) of Regulation (EU, EURATOM) No 966/2012, op. cit.

[118] See Article 318 TFEU. The Commission has so far published four of such reports (see COM (2012) 40 of 17 February 2012; COM (2012) 675 of 21 November 2012; COM (2013) 461 of 26 June 2013 and COM (2014) 383 of 26 June 2014). It should be noted that this new requirement originates from the works of the European Convention (2002-2003). This insertion was opposed at that time by the Commission's representatives on feasibility grounds (see http://european-convention.europa.eu/Docs/Treaty/pdf/892/Art%20III%20310%20Barnier%20FR.pdf).

[119] See footnote 117.

policy achievements remain outside the scope of Directors-General annual activity reports as the Commission considers that they should remain fully in line with its financial responsibility for implementing the EU budget.[120] Hence, these reports focus on funds disbursement, on an assessment of member states' management and control systems and on compliance of spending with the eligibility rules.

- The evaluation reports on the Union's finances provide some indication as to the effectiveness and efficiency of the programmes, but they are not conclusive concerning the expected final results or impacts achieved by EU funds. For example, almost 60% of the EU budget expenditure estimated in 2014 and 2015 is meant to contribute to the Europe 2020 strategy, the EU's long-term growth and jobs plan. It is not possible, however, to single out the contribution expected by each of the programmes (above all Cohesion policy, the most important investment vehicle of this strategy) in achieving Europe 2020 targets.[121] The evaluation reports are therefore not suitable for their intended use in the discharge procedure whereby Parliament, acting on a recommendation from the Council, decides whether to give discharge to the Commission for the implementation of the budget. In particular, Parliament's expectation is clarity and transparency about "the relation between the key performance indicators, their legal/political basis, the amount of expenditure and the results achieved". It recently regretted that "instead of focusing on the achievement of the Union's main objectives, the Commission provided a range of evaluation summaries covering European Union programmes".[122] The last evaluation report on the Union's finances,

---

[120] See European Commission, COM (2014) 342, Brussels, 11 June 2014, p. 4.

[121] Europe 2020 is based on five EU targets to be met by 2020, measured by ten headline indicators. EU and national targets are available in the data tables published by Eurostat (see http://epp.eurostat.ec.europa.eu/portal/page/portal/europe_2020_indicators/headline_indicators). For an analysis of the strategy four years after its launch see, European Commission, "Taking stock of the Europe 2020 strategy for smart, sustainable and inclusive growth", COM (2014) 130 of 19 March 2014.

[122] See European Parliament, Resolution of 10 May 2011 with observations forming an integral part of the Decisions on discharge in respect of the implementation of the general budget of the European Union for the financial year 2009, Section III – Commission and executive agencies, paragraph 200, and Resolution of 3 April 2014

published in June 2014, follows the pattern of the previous ones. However, it provides a description of the monitoring, reporting and evaluation frameworks for the financial programmes in 2014-2020 as well as an outline of which type of information can be expected at different points in time.

In the absence of reliable information on results, the discharge process is focused on compliance issues, notably on the estimate of the level of irregularities and on the financial measures taken by the Commission to mitigate the impact of such irregularities. The use of funds according to 'value for money' principles remains largely outside the scope of this procedure, in contrast with the new provisions introduced by the Treaty of Lisbon.

Despite the Commission's claim that the 2014-2020 programming period will ensure more focus on performance, the use of results indicators will most likely be rather limited. Not least because of a lack of critical mass allowing EU programmes to achieve definite results by themselves. This context puts at risk the possibility of demonstrating that EU funds, in line with the subsidiarity principle, provide an additional value to that which would have been otherwise created by member states' actions alone, thus making a real difference.

The Commission is currently working on a stronger and more coherent framework for monitoring, evaluation and reporting on the performance of EU financial programmes for the on-going MFF, with the purpose of allowing reporting on performance by March 2015. The Commission admits, however, that a "progressive development of a performance culture will take several years to come to full effect, partly because new statistical and other tools need to be developed".[123] On the success of these initiatives will depend the possibility for the Commission to put in place an adequate accountability framework, and therefore a critical condition for a full legitimacy of EU revenue.

It should be stressed that progress will not depend in further reporting arrangements, but rather in making them more meaningful. This would

---

with observations forming an integral part of the decision on discharge in respect of the implementation of the general budget of the European Union for the financial year 2012, Section III – Commission and executive agencies, paragraph 314.

[123] See European Court of Auditors, "Annual Report concerning the financial year 2012", Commission's reply to paragraph 10.1.

require the Commission, entrusted by the Treaties to "execute the budget and manage programmes", "on its own responsibility",[124] to take ownership for the information reported and therefore to have in place a monitoring process aimed at a systematic review of objectives set. This also in view of taking corrective actions when needed and when it is still time, being aware that a possible ex-post disallowance of EU funding through financial corrections will not repair the failure of not having achieved what was initially intended.[125] Moreover, these measures rarely imply a recovery of funds from the beneficiaries, so that they end up most of the time in shifting the burden on national budgets, resulting therefore in a further charge on taxpayers.

The ultimate objective should be that just as the Union cannot adopt any act likely to have appreciable implications for the budget "without providing an assurance that the expenditure arising from such an act is capable of being financed within the limit of the Union's own resources" and in compliance with the MFF,[126] a similar assurance should exist as a prerequisite concerning the setting of "specific, measurable, achievable, relevant and timed objectives" (SMART), to be monitored by performance indicators.[127] This assurance should be part of the assessment required by the subsidiarity principle to conclude whether the objectives of the action envisaged can "be better achieved at Union level".[128]

How much money for the EU budget ?

Since resources are limited and are needed for many essential purposes, there are opportunity costs. The EU and its member states compete for the same revenues. As discussed earlier, one of the characteristics of EU actions

---

[124] See Articles 17(1) TEU and 317 TFEU.

[125] I refer in this respect to the distinction between a 'police patrol' and 'fire alarm' approach, in the meaning of active and passive forms of oversight, as discussed in a previous study (see Cipriani, 2010, the section "Financial corrections: A shortcut for accountability"). The advantage of 'police patrol' oversight is that the actor is under continuous and direct control, while in a 'fire alarm' framework there is less active and direct intervention.

[126] See Article 310(4) TFEU.

[127] As required by Article 30(3) of the Financial Regulation No. 966/2012, op. cit.

[128] See Article 5(3) TEU.

is to be 'inevitable' in view of reaching a better result (criteria of need-for-action or the subsidiarity principle). The underlying logic is that for every EU action, one should be able to answer convincingly the question: Why Europe?

The starting point of any EU action should therefore be a clear definition of the nature and scale of the problem and its originating causes. This is the role of 'impact assessments' undertaken by the European Commission to set objectives related to the issues at stake, to identify possible policy options (including the 'no-action' option) by assessing on a comparative basis their potential impact in addressing the problem, and finally to specify appropriate monitoring and evaluation arrangements for the action proposed.[129]

To achieve its specific objectives, the EU has different means at its disposal – above all, EU law, which is at the root of a significant (and growing) part of national legislation and it is therefore instrumental in bringing different national laws in line with each other and effecting changes in the member countries' basic economic, social and political structures. For example, it has been observed that the strongest generators of economic expansion are most likely to be found in the regulatory sphere. The important engines for this development are the internal market, the monetary union and the growing mobility of skills and knowledge. In stimulating lasting growth, the EU's rules matter more than the EU's expenditures.[130]

To what extent a given EU policy needs EU spending typically requires identifying why this may be necessary (as opposed, for instance, to a simple regulatory initiative and/or purely national spending). What lessons have been learned from previous similar programmes? Are the funds available proportionate to such objectives (in particular, will they ensure a critical mass)? And, what delivery costs (notably administrative burdens) would be entailed?

---

[129] See European Commission, "Impact assessment guidelines", SEC (2009) 92, Brussels, 15 January 2009. See also European Court of Auditors, Special Report No. 3/2010, "Impact assessments in the EU institutions: Do they support decision-making?", Luxembourg, 2010; and O. Fritsch, C. Radaelli, L. Schrefler and A. Renda, "Regulatory quality in the European Commission and the UK: Old questions and new findings", CEPS Working Document, CEPS, Brussels, 26 January 2012.

[130] See Núñez Ferrer (2012).

Naturally, the decision whether the expected added value would justify EU spending is ultimately the result of a political process. This means that the principle of subsidiarity can be considered as a kind of 'political' ceiling to decide 'what' the EU budget should fund and 'how'.[131] In practice, however, the expression of such 'political' ceiling is translated into a 'quantitative' ceiling, with member states agreeing from the outset an overall limit to the resources for the EU budget.[132] Hence, the 'own resources' ceiling represents the main driver of the MFF negotiation, dominated by a 'quantitative' macro-approach at Heading level. Resources are allocated to spending programmes as a result of quantitative arbitrage among policies, rather than as a result of an assessment of the cost of each programme by reference to specific objectives. One example is provided by Cohesion, where there is an allocation of funds, but without specific objectives and targets to be achieved.

As shown lastly by the MFF 2014-2020 negotiation, there could be a significant difference between the appropriations proposed by the Commission and what is ultimately decided. This has been in particular the case for the Headings 'Economic, social and territorial cohesion' (-€54 billion, or –14%), 'Security and citizenship' (-€3 billion, or –17%), and 'Global Europe' (-€11 billion, or –16%). A 'quantitative' approach to EU expenditure will objectively encourage making the necessary adjustments for the programmes concerned through a simple across-the-board reduction of

---

[131] An early definition of the criteria of need-for-action applied to the EU budget can be found in the concept of 'compulsory' and 'non-compulsory' expenditure. This concept goes back to Article 203(4) EEC (as modified by the Treaty of 22 April 1970) that referred to "expenditure necessarily resulting from this Treaty or from acts adopted in accordance therewith", other expenditure being considered consequently as non-compulsory and therefore discretionary. By way of illustration, compulsory expenditure used to cover Agriculture expenditure, Fisheries policy, International agreements concluded with third countries, certain compulsory staffing costs, legal expenses, damages and the monetary reserve. By contrast, the following were classified as non-compulsory expenditure: Structural funds, Financial support in the fields of Energy, Industry and Research. Such distinction has been removed by the Treaty of Lisbon of 2007. By comparison, only around one-third of the 2014-20 MFF could be considered as 'compulsory expenditure'.

[132] For example, similarly to what happened for the previous MFF 2007-2013, five member states (France, Germany, Finland, the Netherlands and the United Kingdom) made known to the Commission in December 2010, before the latter was due to present its proposal of MFF, their desire to have a 'real-terms freeze' on EU expenditure after 2013.

funding (with the risk of further compounding the current lack of critical mass discussed earlier), rather than by re-assessing the objectives of these programmes.

There is actually not such an 'ideal' or 'normal' size for the EU budget: resources equivalent to 1% of EU GNI could be too many, or too few. It all depends on the targets set for the different policies that the Union decides to pursue.

One could well understand that EU expenditure cannot run at full gallop and that therefore some limits to resources should be set. Yet, 'budgetary discipline' cannot represent an end in itself and certainly not a means to guarantee 'value for money'. This is even less so when most programmes continue to be set on the basis of geographically pre-allocated financial envelopes, making spending an objective in itself. The question is whether limits on expenditure may be set not at macro level but by starting from an assessment, at programme level, of the own merits and costs of the different policies to be considered for EU funding. In particular, the MFF negotiation could take advantage of the outcome of impact assessments concerning the lessons of the past, different alternatives and estimated costing of the objectives proposed.

An approach based on establishing first a rationale about what is actually intended to be achieved and the costs involved for the expected results would prepare the ground for more-effective achievements and accountability. Expenditure would be linked from the outset to specific objectives and performance indicators, ensuring that it will be possible later on to measure the impacts of EU spending. Assessing the potential impact of spending programmes would also provide the opportunity to identify potential direct and indirect beneficiaries, in view of resolving possible budgetary imbalances "by means of expenditure policy" rather than by complex correction mechanisms.[133]

In such a framework, the overall resources needed by the EU budget would naturally be determined by the sum of the costs of these policies, as a result of the objectives to be achieved. Should this overall amount appear 'excessive', it would be easier to cut specific objectives of a lower priority rather than making indiscriminate across-the-board reductions. Moreover, to combine predictability and flexibility, consideration could be given to

---

[133] See footnote 23.

allocating to multi-annual programmes amounts 'deemed necessary', representing an indicative estimate of the budgetary implications with possibly minimum and maximum amounts, instead of the current fixed financial envelopes.[134]

This process could reconcile the legitimate objective of setting some expenditure limits with good management of the programmes. In particular, it would allow adapting the size of programmes (upwards but also downwards) during implementation, for example by the middle of the MFF, according to expected results and lessons learned as well as following new priorities. As pointed out by Parliament, "it is particularly important that allocations of funds are based on objective criteria and on a continuous evaluation of their performance".[135] By the way, the idea of a mid-term review/revision is already provided for in the 2014-2020 MFF, even if there is no expectation that pre-allocated national envelopes will be amended by such review. The fluctuation of EU VAT revenue according to economic circumstances, as sketched in the section "Making the VAT-resource visible to citizens", would go in the same direction.

A MFF as the consolidation of an assessment programme by programme would be in line with the evolution of the balance of powers between Council and Parliament, taking account of the fact that almost all EU legislation is to be endorsed by both institutions through the ordinary legislative procedure. The process suggested would lead in practice to align the powers for approving the MFF with those for approving the spending programmes. Such process would also make the annual budgetary procedure more meaningful, as opposed to a transposition of the MFF annual estimates. This would be a natural development of the extension of the co-decision framework for approving the annual budget where Parliament is at an equal level with the Council.

Concluding remarks

A reform of EU revenue cannot lose sight of the expenditure side of the budget. Irrespective of the visibility of its funding source, the basis for

---

[134] The concept of 'means deemed necessary' is used for the specific programmes developed within each activity of the multiannual Research framework programme (see article 182(3) TFEU).

[135] See European Parliament, Resolution of 25 March 2009 on the Mid-Term Review of the 2007-2013 Financial Framework, paragraph 16.

legitimacy of EU revenue lies in the possibility to convincingly demonstrate whether and to what extent EU expenditure has met the expectations and produced tangible and positive results for Europeans. It is this demonstration that can make citizens accept the corresponding taxation. In the current weak accountability context, notably for performance, a visible fiscal source for the EU budget has actually the potential to enhance trust in the EU's finances by increasing the pressure to demonstrate the European added value of EU expenditure.

A relevant assessment of performance would require the design of spending programmes in terms of specific, measurable and achievable objectives, expected outcomes and resulting costs. Yet, EU spending programmes pursue a multiplicity of grand objectives, often unrelated to the available funding and with no specific expected achievements. Also, EU spending programmes are either entitlement programmes where beneficiaries only have to meet certain conditions (like direct payments to farmers) or 'input'-based, so EU disbursements are only linked to the 'eligibility' of the expenditure incurred. Moreover, the 'geographical' allocation of most EU expenditure makes 'spending' an implicit objective and possibly the main one.

There is currently no reliable system for collecting performance data in order to identify and report on results and impacts, as they become available. Due to the absence of a 'battery indicator', the Commission's reporting has failed so far to provide sufficient, relevant and reliable evidence on what the EU's expenditure has achieved. Yet, weak information on performance has a knock-on effect on the annual discharge procedure, meant to be more than a formal act of closing the accounts, focused as it is on compliance issues whilst it should offer the political authorities "an opportunity to assess the management of the financial resources of the European Union, to propose measures for its improvement and to express an overall political judgment on its quality".[136]

The 'own resources' ceiling represents the main driver of the MFF negotiation. Resources are allocated to spending programmes as a result of quantitative arbitrage among policy areas, rather than following an assessment of the cost of each programme by reference to specific objectives. An approach based on establishing first a rationale about what it is actually intended to achieve and the costs involved for the expected results would

---

[136] See European Parliament, Resolution of 13 December 2000 on reform of budgetary control procedures and institutions, paragraph D.

prepare the ground for more effective achievements and accountability. Expenditure would be linked from the outset to specific objectives and performance indicators, making it possible later on to measure the impacts of EU spending and report there upon.

In such a framework, the overall resources needed by the EU budget would naturally be determined by the sum of the costs of these policies, as a result of the objectives to be achieved. Moreover, to combine predictability and flexibility, consideration could be given to allocating to multi-annual programmes amounts 'deemed necessary', representing an indicative estimate of the budgetary implications with possibly minimum and maximum amounts, instead of the current fixed financial envelopes. This process would allow adapting the size of programmes (upwards but also downwards) during implementation, for example by the middle of the MFF, according to expected results and lessons learned as well as in response to emerging new priorities. As a result, the importance of the annual budget procedure will be enhanced.

A MFF, as the consolidation of an assessment programme by programme, would be in line with the evolution of the balance of powers between Council and Parliament, taking account of the broad co-decision framework for approving the spending programmes and the annual budget, where Parliament is now on an equal level with the Council.

REFERENCES

Abritta, L., D. Ballanti, R. Convenevole, C. Equizzi and S. Pisani (2003), "Gli effetti dell'applicazione degli studi di settore nel biennio 1998-99", Agenzia delle Entrate, November (www1.agenziaentrate.gov.it/ufficiostudi/pdf/2003/effetti%20applicazione%20studi%20settore.pdf).

Cipriani, G. (2007), *Rethinking the EU Budget: Three Unavoidable Reforms*, CEPS Paperback, CEPS, Brussels, November.

_____ (2010), *The EU Budget: Responsibility without accountability?*, CEPS Paperback, CEPS, Brussels, November.

Cipriani, G. and S. Pisani (2004), "The European budget: An alternative to budgetary balances to assess benefits for the member states", Working Paper No. 339, Società italiana di economia pubblica, Pavia, October (www.siepweb.it/siep/images/joomd/1399116284339.pdf).

Convenevole, R. (2011), Come approdare al regime definitivo dell'IVA nell'Unione Europea (www.ilmiolibro.it).

_____ (2011), *La materia oscura dell'IVA* (www.ilmiolibro.it).

Ehlermann, C.D. (1982), "The Financing of the Community: The distinction between financial contributions and own resources", *Common Market Law Review*, Vol. 19, No. 4.

European Commission (1965), "Financement de la politique agricole commune – Ressources propres de la Communauté – Renforcement des pouvoirs du Parlement européen", COM (65) 150, Brussels, 31 March.

_____ (1987), "Report on the Financing of the Community Budget", COM (87) 101, Brussels, 28 February.

_____ (1996), "A common system of VAT, A programme for the Single Market", COM (96) 328, Brussels, 22 July.

_____ (1997), "Budget Contributions, EU Expenditure, Budgetary Balances and Relative Prosperity of the Member States", paper presented by President Santer to the Ecofin Council, 13 October (http://aei.pitt.edu/40266/1/A4661.pdf).

_____ (1998), "Financing the European Union", Commission report on the operation of the own resources system, COM (1998) 560, Brussels, 7 October.

_____ (2002), "A project for the European Union", COM (2002) 247, Brussels, 22 May.

_____ (2004), "Building our common future: Policy challenges and budgetary means of the enlarged Union 2007–13", COM (2004) 101, Brussels, 26 February.

_____ (2004), "Report on the use of administrative cooperation arrangements in the fight against VAT fraud", COM (2004) 260, Brussels, 16 April.

_____ (2004), "Financing the European Union, Commission report on the operation of the own resources system", Vols. I and II, COM (2004) 505 final, Brussels, 14 July.

_____ (2008), "Reforming the Budget, Changing Europe: Short Summary of Contributions", SEC (2008) 2739, Brussels, 3 November.

_____ (2009), "Impact assessment guidelines", SEC (2009) 92, Brussels, 15 January.

_____ (2010), "The EU Budget review, Technical annexes", SEC (2010) 7000, Brussels, 19 October.

_____ (2010), "Towards a simpler, more robust and efficient VAT system", COM (2010) 695, Brussels, 1 December.

_____ (2011), "A Budget for Europe 2020", COM (2011) 500, Brussels, 29 June.

_____ (2011), Proposal for a Council Decision on the system of own resources of the European Union, COM (2011) 510, Brussels, 29 June.

_____ (2011), Proposal for a Council Directive on a common system of financial transaction tax and amending Directive 2008/7/EC, COM (2011) 594, Brussels, 28 September.

_____ (2011), Amended proposal for a Council Decision on the system of own resources of the European Union, COM (2011) 739, Brussels, 9 November.

_____ (2011), "The added value of the EU budget", SEC (2011) 867 final, Brussels, 29 June.

_____ (2011) "Financing the EU budget: Report on the operation of the own resources system", SEC (2011) 876, Brussels, 27 October.

_____ (2012), "Report on the evaluation of the Union's finances based on the results achieved", COM (2012) 40, Brussels, 17 February.

_____ (2012), "Report on the evaluation of the Union's finances based on the results achieved", COM (2012) 675, Brussels, 21 November.

_____ (2013), Proposal for a Council Directive implementing enhanced cooperation in the area of financial transaction tax, Brussels, COM (2013) 71 of 14 February.

_____ (2013) Commission recommendation of 12 March 2013 on enhancing the democratic and efficient conduct of the elections to the European Parliament, OJ L 79 of 21 March.

_____ (2013),"Report on the evaluation of the Union's finances based on the results achieved", COM (2013) 461, Brussels, 26 June.

_____ (2013), "European Research area progress report 2013", COM (2013) 637, Brussels, 20 September.

_____ (2014), "Seventh report under Article 12 of Regulation (EEC, Euratom) n° 1553/89 on VAT collection and control procedures," COM (2014) 69, Brussels, 12 February.

_____ (2014), "Taking stock of the Europe 2020 strategy for smart, sustainable and inclusive growth", COM (2014) 130, Brussels, 19 March.

_____ (2014), "Working document on calculation, financing, payment and entry in the budget of the correction of budgetary imbalances in favour of the United Kingdom", COM (2014) 271, Brussels, 14 May.

_____ (2014), "Taxation trends in the European Union", Luxembourg, 2014.

_____ (2014), "Synthesis of the Commission's management achievements in 2013", COM (2014) 342, Brussels, 11 June.

_____ (2014), "Report on the evaluation of the Union's finances based on the results achieved", COM (2014) 383, Brussels, 26 June.

European Council (1984), Conclusions of the Session of the European Council at Fontainebleau, 25-26 June.

_____ (1999), Presidency Conclusions of the Berlin European Council of 24-25 March.

European Court of Auditors (1998), Special Report No. 6/98, "The Court's assessment of the system of resources based on VAT and GNP", OJ No. C 241 of 31 July.

_____ (2010), Special Report No. 3/2010, "Impact assessments in the EU institutions: Do they support decision-making?" (www.eca.europa.eu).

_____ (2011), Annual Report concerning the financial year 2010, OJ No. C 326 of 10 November.

_____ (2012), Special Report No. 12/2012, "Did the Commission and Eurostat improve the process for producing reliable and credible European statistics?", (www.eca.europa.eu).

_____ (2012), Opinion No. 2/2012 of 20 March 2012, OJ No. C 112 of 18 April.

_____ (2013), Special Report No. 11/2013, "Getting the Gross National Income (GNI) data right: A more structured and better-focused approach would improve the effectiveness of the Commission's verification" (www.eca.europa.eu).

_____ (2013), Annual Report concerning the financial year 2012, OJ No. C 331 of 14 November.

European Parliament (1981), Resolution of 9 April 1981 on the Community's own resources.

_____ (1994), "Report on the System of Own Resources in the European Union", A3-0228/94, Rapporteur: H. Langes, 8 April.

_____ (1994) Resolution of 21 April 1994 on a new system of own resources for the European Union.

_____ (2005) Resolution of 8 June 2005 on Policy Challenges and Budgetary Means of the Enlarged Union 2007–2013.

_____ (2007) Resolution of 29 March 2007 on the future of the European Union's own resources.

_____ (2007) Resolution of 24 April 2007 with comments forming an integral part of the decision on the discharge for implementation of the

European Union general budget for the financial year 2005, Section III – Commission.

_____ (2009) Resolution of 25 March 2009 on the Mid-Term Review of the 2007-2013 Financial Framework.

_____ (2009) Resolution of 25 March 2009 on the ABB-ABM method as a management tool for allocating budgetary resources.

_____ (2010) Resolution of 15 June 2010 on the mandate for the trilogue on the 2011 draft budget.

_____ (2011) Resolution of 10 May 2011 with observations forming an integral part of the Decisions on discharge in respect of the implementation of the general budget of the European Union for the financial year 2009, Section III – Commission and executive agencies.

_____ (2011) Resolution of 8 June 2011 on Investing in the future: a new Multiannual Financial Framework (MFF) for a competitive, sustainable and inclusive Europe.

_____ (2012) Resolution of 23 May 2012 on the proposal for a Council directive on a common system of financial transaction tax and amending Directive 2008/7/EC.

_____ (2012) Resolution of 13 June 2012 on the Multiannual Financial Framework and own resources.

_____ (2012) Resolution of 23 October 2012 in the interests of achieving a positive outcome of the Multiannual Financial Framework 2014-2020 approval procedure.

_____ (2013) Resolution of 21 May 2013 on the Annual Tax Report: how to free the EU potential for economic growth.

_____ (2013) Resolution of 3 July 2013 on the proposal for a Council directive implementing enhanced cooperation in the area of financial transaction tax.

_____ (2013) Resolution of 3 July 2013 on the political agreement on the Multiannual Financial Framework 2014-2020.

_____ (2013) Resolution of 12 December 2013 on the call for a measurable and binding commitment against tax evasion and tax avoidance in the EU.

_____ (2014) Resolution of 3 April 2014 with observations forming an integral part of the decision on discharge in respect of the implementation of the general budget of the European Union for the financial year 2012, Section III – Commission and executive agencies.

Fritsch, O., C. Radaelli, L. Schrefler and A. Renda (2012), "Regulatory quality in the European Commission and the UK: Old questions and new findings", CEPS Working Document, CEPS, Brussels, 26 January (www.ceps.eu/book/regulatory-quality-european-commission-and-uk-old-questions-and-new-findings).

Gros, D. and S. Micossi (2005), "A Better Budget for the European Union", CEPS Policy Brief No. 66, CEPS, Brussels, February.

Heinemann, F., P. Mohl and S. Osterloh (2008), "Reform Options for the Own Resources System", Centre for European Economic Research (ZEW), Mannheim.

Jenkins, R. (1977), Speech by Commission President Jenkins to the European Parliament, 11 January.

Keen, M., R. Krelove and J. Norregaard (2010), "The Financial Activities Tax", in S. Claessens, M. Keen and C. Pazarbasioglu (eds), *Financial Sector Taxation, The IMF's Report to the G-20 and Background Material*, International Monetary Fund, Washington, D.C., September.

Mortensen, J., J. Núñez Ferrer and F. Infelise (2014), "How do members states handle contributions to the EU budget in their national budgets", study undertaken for the European Parliament's Committee on Budgets, October (www.europarl.europa.eu/RegData/etudes/STUD/2014/490686/IPOL_STU(2014)490686_EN.pdf).

Núñez Ferrer, J. (2012), *Investing where it matters: An EU budget for long-term growth*, CEPS Task Force Report, CEPS, Brussels.

Núñez Ferrer, J. and M. Katarivas (2014), "What are the effects of the EU budget: Driving force or drop in the ocean?", CEPS Special Report, No. 86, CEPS, Brussels, April.

Pisani, S. (2014), "Tax gap and the performance of Italian Revenue Agency: An ongoing project", Presentation at the International Tax Analysis Conference 2014, 20-21 January, London (www.esrc.ac.uk/hmrc/images/6a-tax-gap-and-the-performance-of-italian-revenue-agency_tcm19-29916.pdf).

Strasser, D. (1991), "The Finances of Europe: The budgetary and financial law of the European Communities", Luxembourg: Office of Official Publications of the European Communities.

Tarschys, D. (2005), "The Enigma of European Added Value", SIEPS Report No. 4, Swedish Institute for European Policy Studies, Stockholm, June.

Tremonti, G. and G. Vitaletti (1991), *La fiera delle tasse*, Bologna: Il Mulino.

INDEX

www.ingramcontent.com/pod-product-compliance
Lightning Source LLC
Chambersburg PA
CBHW050538270326
41926CB00015B/3282